PANCHATANTRA

PANCHATANTRA

PANDIT VISHNU SHARMA

Translated by
G. L. Chandiramani

Rupa & Co

Copyright © Sheila G. Chandiramani

First in Rupa Paperback 1991
Twentieth Impression 2011

Published by
Rupa Publications India Pvt. Ltd.
7/16, Ansari Road, Daryaganj,
New Delhi 110 002

Sales Centres:

Allahabad Bengaluru Chennai
Hyderabad Jaipur Kathmandu
Kolkata Mumbai

Typeset by
Mindways Design
1410 Chiranjiv Tower
43 Nehru Place
New Delhi 110 019

Printed in India by
Gopsons Papers Ltd.
A-14 Sector 60
Noida 201 301

PREFACE

The original text of the *Panchatantra* in Sanskrit was probably written about 200 B.C. by a great Hindu scholar, Pandit Vishnu Sharma. But some of the tales themselves must be much older, their origin going back to the period of the Rig-Veda and Upanishads (from 1500 B.C. to 500 B.C.). According to some scholars of the Indo-European languages, the *Panchatantra* is the oldest collection of Indian fables surviving.

In course of time, travellers took these stories with them to Persia and Arabia and finally through Greece, they reached Europe. It is surmised that a version of the *Panchatantra* was composed in the Pahlavi language of pre-Islamic Iran sometime in the 6th century A.D., being followed by an Arabic one in the 8th century A.D. The Greek translation was made towards the close of the 11th century A.D. from which it was translated into various European languages. This accounts for the fact that to many/ Westerners, some of the stories have a familiar ring. So far it has been translated into 50 or more languages of the world.

The gypsies, whose Indian origin is well established, also helped in spreading these tales in Europe.

The *Panchatantra* is essentially connected with one of the branches of science known by the Indians as the 'Nitishastra' which in Sanskrit means 'A book of wise conduct in life'. It attempts to teach us, how to understand people, how to choose reliable and trustworthy friends, how to meet difficulties and solve problems through tact and wisdom, and how to live in peace and harmony in the face of hypocrisy, deceit and many pitfalls in life.

The *Panchatantra* is woven round the frame of a tale of a king who entrusts his three 'dud' sons to a learned man, a Brahmin, called Pandit Vishnu Sharma, to enlighten their minds within six months. The Brahmin promises to educate them and takes them to his 'ashrama' (hermitage). There he recites to them his specially composed tales divided into five tantras (in Sanskrit: Pancha=five and tantra=systems or parts) of how to deal with people in life.

The language of the author is both artistic and elegant. The tale is narrated in prose while the exposition of a philosophical and moral theme is put in verse; maxims or wise sayings are also expressed in verse, which either sums up the narration or introduces the next tale.

The story-teller's art sugars the pill of his sober philosophy. He sets story within story and keeps us waiting for the sequels and so leads us on through the five 'tantras.' As one fable follows another, people and animals are constantly changing places, and they share the same characteristics of love and hatred, compassion and wit, selfless courage and base cowardice, generosity and meanness. Each story has a moral and philosophical theme which has stood the test of time and so is true even in modern times — an age of atomic fear and madness.

The *Panchatantra* is a rare book, for in no book will you find philosophy, psychology, politics, music. astronomy, human relationship, etc., all discussed together in such a simple and yet elegant style. This is exactly what Pandit Vishnu Sharma had in mind, to give as much knowledge to the princes as possible. And no doubt not only the princes but also millions of listeners and readers for the last 2,200 years have benefited from this most unique book.

The book is intended for the adult mind, though children will love it if helped; it contains a fountain of India's philosophical wisdom — a fountain of nectar.

G. L. Chandiramani

TRANSLATOR'S NOTE

Despite my own strong conviction that the *Panchatantra* has a vital message for the world today, I would probably never have undertaken the translation of the *Panchatantra* into English and German had it not been for the encouragement of my "guru", Professor (Dr.) S.B. Hudlikar (Heidelberg, W. Germany).

Perhaps similar attempts have been made by men of superior talent and wisdom, but I have made a modest attempt, working on the text for seven years, to bring out a translation in modern English which would remain true to the spirit of the Sanskrit text, though I have been highly conscious of my own inadequacies in the face of such a task.

The present form of the Sanskrit text, subjected as it has been, over the ages, to constant revision and adaptation, presents a sizeable problem to any would-be translator.

Several illogicalities and non-sequiturs seem to have crept into the text with the passage of time, naturally enough, when one considers that, until modern times, these stories have been for telling, rather than reading, and they have been told time and again all over India and in many parts of the world, each story-teller using his own particular artistry to beguile his listeners, adding a little detail here and there, as he thought fit. So it is that, from the reader's point of view, sometimes the construction of the text is weak (for instance, the fifth tantra is loosely constructed and incomplete; Chakradhara's story ends abruptly and we never do return to the Brahmin's wife or the judges who were telling these stories).

The present translation attempts to reproduce as accurately as possible the Sanskrit text in English but in a logical and readable form. In the interests of continuity, short sections have been omitted, sentences rearranged and, occasionally, a linking sentence added. But every attempt has been made to keep such amendments to the minimum, though keeping in view, at the same time, to retain the flavour of the original text, which is both artistic and elegant.

All the Sanskrit names, designations and exclamations have been retained in the translation to preserve the Indian atmosphere and tradition of the book. The writer, Pandit Vishnu Sharma, seems to have chosen the names with great care, for everywhere they have got some definite relationship to the character or incident in the story. At several places, there is a distinct significance or satire in the meaning of the Sanskrit names. I would therefore request the reader to refer to *glossary*. I hope it will help him towards a thorough understanding of this ancient Indian Classic to enable more enjoyable reading.

The glossary has been provided for reference at the end of the book. The pronunciations of the Sanskrit words are comparatively simple if each word is split into syllables and then pronounced.

My desire is to establish a direct relationship with the reader. I would welcome comments and criticisms — they will help me to improve upon the present translation when bringing out the next edition.

The present translation is the result of the talent, excellent team-work and experience of my friends who have affectionately guided me. They are all experts in their own respective fields.

Above all, Goddess Saraswati has smiled on me, and it is to her that I humbly dedicate this book.

For my own part, I claim no credit. I have simply performed the task of a bee that collects honey from fragrant flowers.

ACKNOWLEDGEMENTS

I am indebted to my "ξυru", Professor (Dr.) S.B. Hudlikar (Heidelberg, W. Germany), Director of European Languages, Bombay, for not only encouraging me to undertake the translation of the *Panchatantra* into English and German but also for guiding me through the various Sanskrit versions, giving me benefit of his experience in translating and his scholarly knowledge of the Sanskrit language.

I express my deep sense of gratitude to Dr. A. Karl (Vienna, Austria) for going through the manuscript, scrutinising it word by word, and for making many useful suggestions. He has also corrected my German translation of the *Panchatantra*.

Miss Sylvia Gidley, B.A. (Wales), began correcting the English manuscript in London, but was so fascinated by its contents that she was lured to come to India and complete it. Without her, the translation would have become drab and lifeless.

And my brother (Amolak L. Chandiramani) has been very enthusiastic about my work right from the beginning. He minutely went through the proofs several times and his suggestions were exceedingly useful in improving the language of the book.

CONTENTS

PANCHATANTRA

Once upon a time, in the south of India, there was a city called Mahilaropyam.* A king by the name of Amarshakti* lived there. He was a very learned man and extremely accomplished in various arts and skills.

The king had three sons called Bahushakti*, Ugrashakti* and Anantashakti*, who were complete duds and had no interest whatsoever in studying. Realising this, the king assembled his ministers and addressed them in these words, "Gentlemen, you already know how ignorant my sons are. They have no understanding whatsoever. Looking at them I cannot enjoy my kingdom. As they say:

'Unborn, dead and stupid sons,
The first two are to be preferred
For they cause sorrow only once
Whilst stupid sons are a torment to the heart
Till the end of life.'

And,

'What is the good of a cow
That neither bears a calf nor gives milk?
And, what is the good of a son
Who is neither enlightened nor devoted?'

—"So please tell me ways and means by which my sons would be enlightened."

One of the ministers replied, "Your Majesty! Twelve years are spent in learning grammar alone and then the required sciences, economics, religion and sexology are so vast that it takes a long time to master them. And only then the intelligence is awakened."

But a minister, a man called Sumati*, said, "Our life is transitory and these sciences take too long to master them. So we must find a shorter way to enlighten the minds of the princes. I know of a Brahmin*, called

---

* All asterisked words explained in the Glossary at the end.

Vishnu Sharma*, who is an expert in all the sciences and has earned an excellent reputation among his innumerable disciples. So I suggest that the princes should be handed over to him. He will certainly instruct them very well."

When the king heard this, he had Vishnu Sharma invited to the palace and said to him, "Bhagawan*, please educate my sons quickly in nitishastras*. I shall be so grateful to you. I shall present you with a hundred tax-free villages."

This was the reply that Vishnu Sharma made to the king. "Your Majesty, please listen to what I have to say. Believe me, it's the truth. I would not like to sell my wisdom out of greed for money but if I have not made your sons thorough in nitishastras within six months, then I am ready to forfeit my name. Hear my lion's roar*. I don't crave for wealth. I am almost eighty years old and have all my desires under control. Now, would you please make a note of today's date. If I have not educated your sons in nitishastras within six months, then I do not deserve a place in heaven."

The king and his ministers were surprised as well as pleased to hear this seemingly impossible resolution. With great appreciation and respect, the king handed over his sons to the Brahmin and felt at ease.

After taking the princes to his ashrama*, Vishnu Sharma began to recite to them his specially composed stories, divided into five tantras*.

1. Conflict amongst friends.
2. Winning of friends.
3. Crows and owls.
4. The forfeit of profits.
5. Action without due consideration.

Now they say:

"A man who has studied this nitishastra
Or listened to its precepts
Will never be defeated
Not even by Indra*, the Lord of the Heaven."

1
CONFLICT AMONGST FRIENDS

This is the beginning of the first tantra called, "Conflict amongst friends".

"A great friendship had developed in the jungle,
Between the lion and the bullock,
But it was destroyed
By a very wicked and avaricious jackal."

This is how the story goes:

In the south of India there was a city called Mahilaropyam. The son of a very rich merchant lived there. His name was Vardhamanaka*. One night, as he lay awake in bed, his thoughts were troubled. This is what he was turning over in his mind. "Even when a man has plenty of money, it is still a good thing for him to try to make more. As they say:

'There is nothing in life that money cannot achieve,
And so a wise man should be bent on increasing his wealth.
If a man has money, he has friends,
When he has money,
He is recognised by his relatives.
In this world a stranger becomes kinsman to a moneyed man,
Whilst a poor man is avoided even by his family.
A man with money will even be considered a scholar.
Money makes the old young,
But the young grow old for want of it.' "

Vardhamanaka came to a decision. On an auspicious day, he took leave of his elders and made preparations to travel to Mathura* with his wares. He had two bullocks called Sanjivaka* and Nandaka*, both born in his house and able to carry heavy loads. He harnessed them to a cart and set out, accompanied by a few servants.

After a few days, as they reached the bank of the river Yamuna*, one of the bullocks, the one called

Sanjivaka, broke his leg and collapsed. Vardhamanaka
was most distressed to see his bullock in this condition
and for love of Sanjivaka, he called a halt at the place
for three nights.

When the cart drivers saw Vardhamanaka so dejected,
they said to him, "Most noble Sir, why loiter in a jungle
full of lions and tigers for the sake of one ox, when it
may mean sacrificing everything. For they say:

'A wise man should never sacrifice big interests
For smaller ones.' "

When he heard them say this, Vardhamanaka left a
couple of men to look after the injured bullock and set
off on the remainder of the journey.

The following day, these men caught up with him.
They had thought that they may come to some harm
in the jungle and so they lied to Vardhamanaka, "Sir,
Sanjivaka is dead. We burnt him in fire." When he
heard this, Vardhamanaka performed the last rites, out
of gratitude to his devoted servant.

But Sanjivaka was destined to live longer. He ate tender
plants from the bed of the river Yamuna, thereby
regained a little of his strength and somehow managed
to get up. The cool breezes greatly refreshed him. He
ate grass that was green and shining and within a few
days he became fat and strong. It's true what they say:

"He whom fortune smiles on,
Though unprotected, eludes destruction,
But he who has luck against him, is done for,
Even though he be well protected.
A man left defenceless in a jungle survives,
But even after a great struggle to live,
He may die in his own house."

Now in this very jungle there lived a lion called
Pingalaka*, with an entourage of other animals. One
day he was parched with thirst and went to the bank
of the river Yamuna to drink water. There, he heard
from a great distance the hideous roar of Sanjivaka.
Pingalaka was terrified in his heart but outwardly he

hid his feelings and went and sat down under a banyan*
tree. His court gathered round him.

Now Pingalaka had, in his retinue, two jackals called
Karataka* and Damanaka*. They were the sons of his
previous minister but had been dismissed from their
posts and so always followed him at a distance.

When they saw the lion returning without having
quenched his thirst, they began to consult with each
other. "My dear Karataka," said Damanaka, "this master
of ours went to drink water but has returned without
doing so and now he sits under the banyan tree
surrounded by his retinue."

—"What has that to do with us?" said Karataka, for:
  'The man who takes on work
  That was never meant for him,
  Courts destruction,
  Like the monkey who took out the wedge from the
    log.' "

—"How was that?" asked Damanaka.

And Karataka told:

THE STORY OF THE MONKEY AND THE LOG

"A merchant had started building a temple beneath the trees on the outskirts of a town. Every day the carpenters and the workmen used to go into the town for their midday meals. Now, one particular day, a troop of wandering monkeys arrived on the scene. One of the carpenters, who was in the middle of sawing a log, put a wedge in it, to prevent the log from closing up, and then went off.

"The monkeys started playing on the tops of the trees and the high structures, without a care in the world. One poor monkey, not destined to live long, sat down on the half split log, caught hold of the wedge with his hands and started pulling it out. And behold! The wedge came out all of a sudden and the log closed in, but not before the monkey's legs had been trapped in the gap. He was instantly killed.

—"And so," continued Karataka, "that's why I said, that you should never meddle in other people's business. And our business is to eat whatever has been left by the lion."

—"What!" retorted Damanaka. "You think that our only concern is to find food? I don't agree with you, for they say:

'It's despicable crows
That live off whatever is available for eating.' "

—"Anyway," said Karataka, "now that we are no longer in service to the king, why should we bother our heads about it?"

—"No!" retaliated Damanaka. "Don't talk like that, for:

'A man who is not a minister, becomes one
When he serves the king well,
But even a minister can be removed from his post,
If he fails to serve him well.
The servant who pays attention to
What pleases or displeases his lord,

Can even get the upper hand over a wicked master.
And how can a wise man fail to handle a king
When he sees that snakes, tigers, elephants and
  lions
Can be brought under control, one way or
  another!' "

—"So, under the circumstances, what do you propose
to do?" asked Karataka.

—"Today our master and his court are scared out of
their wits," replied Damanaka. "I shall take it upon
myself to find out the cause of their fear. Then I shall
use one of the six Diplomatic Methods, which are:

To make peace or war,
To attack or to entrench,
To take protection under a powerful ally
Or provoke a quarrel between one's opponents."

—"But, how do you know that our master is scared out
of his wits?" asked Karataka.

—"You don't have to know anything," replied Damanaka.
As Manu* said:

'The thoughts of others can be ascertained
In their faces, their gestures, their speech,
And the twitching of their eyes.'

—"And so through the power of my intelligence, I shall
free the terrified Pingalaka from his fear and, at the
same time, get back my position as minister."

—"But you don't know what service means," said
Karataka. "How then will you win him over?"

—"Well," said Damanaka, "while I was playing on my
father's lap, I listened to the fables told by Mahatmas*
and since then I have remembered the substance of
them and have stored them in my mind. Listen:

'Brave men, scholars, and those who know how to
  serve,
Only these collect golden roses on this earth.'

And,

'To serve a king,
Who fails to appreciate the merits of the learned,

Is like ploughing a barren land.' "
—"But, do tell me," said Karataka, "what will you say
to him to begin with?"
—"Whatever I say," said Damanaka, "must be said at
the right time for, even if Brihaspati* himself speaks at
the wrong moment, he will be insulted."
—"But it's so difficult to influence kings", said Karataka.
"They are hard and heartless as the mountains and are
surrounded by wicked people."
—"That is true," said Damanaka, "but:

'If a king is angry he must be flattered.
His friend should be considered a friend,
His enemy, an enemy.
And his presents should be appreciated.
In this way he can be won over without magic.' "

—"If that's the case," said Karataka, "then it's up to
you. May God protect you."

Damanaka bowed, took leave of Karataka and then
went straight to the king. As soon as Pingalaka saw
Damanaka coming, he said to his guard, "Let Damanaka,
the son of my former minister, come in without any
hindrance."

When Damanaka arrived, Pingalaka spoke kindly to
him.

—"Are you happy?" he asked. "Why have you come to
see me after such a long time?"

—"Your Majesty!" replied Damanaka. "Although my
master has no particular work for me, yet I must still
offer my services when the occasion demands. The king
needs all three types of people: High, middle and low.
And they say:

'If the king needs a little stick
To pick his ear or tooth,
How much more does he need a man
Who has hands and the power of speech?'

—"Although we were always with you as your servants,
even followed you in bad times, yet our jobs were taken
away from us. That was unjust on your part and I

blame you, not the man who replaced us, for:
'A king who does not understand the difference
Between glass and diamonds,
Does not deserve to be served.
For how can a person of intelligence
Remain even for a moment
In a place, where men are unable to differentiate
Between right and wrong.
And conversely the servant who deserves to serve,
Is the man who, when honoured, remains humble,
When insulted, keeps a scowl from his face
And thus remains equally detached
From honour and insult.
For kings and servants mutually depend on each
    other:
There can be no king without a servant
And no servant without a king.
When a king is pleased, he gives to his servants
Gold in abundance
And they in return for such honour,
Sacrifice themselves to him.'
—"It is unbefitting that you should think us inferior just because we are jackals, for:
'Silk comes out of the worm,
Gold out of the rocks,
The lotus from filth,
Fire from a piece of wood,
And the gem from the hood of the cobra*.'
—"So, too," continued Damanaka, "virtue can come out of people humbly born."
  Said Pingalaka, "It makes no difference whether you are high or low, you are the son of my former minister, so if you have anything to say, say it without hesitation."
—"Master!" said Damanaka. "Indeed I have something to say."
—"Well then," said Pingalaka, "tell me."
—"But, I must tell you in confidence," said Damanaka, for:

'Whatever is heard by six ears
Can never remain secret,
And so a wise man should not allow his secrets
To reach six ears.' "

The tiger, the wolves and the others understood the
sign that Pingalaka made in response to this and went
away.

Then Damanaka said to the king, "You went to the
river to drink water but you returned without doing so.
Why was that?"

—"Oh, for no particular reason," answered Pingalaka
with a smile.

—"If it's something that you cannot talk about, then so
be it," said Damanaka, for:

'There are some things that you can tell to wives,
Some to sons, some to the family,
But you can't tell everything to everybody.' "

When he heard this, Pingalaka thought to himself,
"The fellow seems deserving enough. I'll take him into
my confidence, for:

'When a man can share his sorrows
With a trusted friend or a devoted servant,
A kind master or a faithful wife,
That man finds relief.' "

So Pingalaka asked Damanaka, "Can you hear that
terrifying noise in the distance?"

—"Yes," replied Damanaka, "I can, what of it?"

—"My friend," said Pingalaka, "I want to get away from
this jungle."

—"Whatever for?" asked Damanaka.

—"Because," replied Pingalaka, "some monstrous animal
has come here and it is he who makes this loud noise.
Probably he is as strong as his voice is loud."

—"You mean that it's just a noise you are afraid of!"
exclaimed Damanaka. "That's not right. For generations
this jungle has belonged to you. It would be wrong for
you to leave it suddenly like that. Besides, there are all
kinds of noises made by drums, conches, Veena* and

so on, so you should never be afraid of a mere noise,
for:

    'When the hungry jackal conquered his fear of a
      noise,
    He found food.' "
—"How was that?" asked Pingalaka.
  And Damanaka told:

THE STORY OF THE JACKAL AND THE DRUM

"There was once a jackal called Gomaya*. One day, he was very hungry and he wandered about in search of food. At last he came to a battlefield. The fighting armies had left behind a drum, lying near some creepers. Because of a strong wind, the creepers were rubbing against the drum and making a noise. When the jackal heard this, he got frightened and thought to himself, 'Unless I can make myself scarce before whoever is making this noise sees me, I am done for. But then, it is unwise to desert one's house suddenly, so instead I must try to find out who is making this noise.'

"So he took all his courage in his hands and as he crept forward he realised that it was only a drum. He continued his search and nearby he found sufficient food to last him a long time.

—"And, so you see," Damanaka went on, "you shouldn't be afraid of a mere noise."

—"How can I be brave," said Pingalaka, "when my whole court is trembling with fright and wants to get away from here?"

—"Master," said Damanaka, "servants should not be held responsible for they only follow their master's example. They say:

'Horses, weapons, books, conversation,
   The harp and a wife,
   They all become worthy or worthless
   According to the man they belong to.'

—"And so," continued Damanaka, "be brave and wait here patiently until I return. I am going to find out about the noise. And then we shall do whatever is for the best."

—"Are you brave enough to go?" asked Pingalaka.

—"Certainly," said Damanaka, "besides, why should a servant ask questions whether a thing is to be done or not, if it is his master's pleasure."

—"My dear friend!" said Pingalaka. "Well, if that's the case, then by all means, go. May God protect you."

Damanaka bowed before the king and set out, following the noise made by Sanjivaka.

After the jackal had taken his leave, Pingalaka got frightened. He sank into a deep reverie and began to think to himself, "I have made a mistake in confiding my intentions to him. As I deprived him of his position, he may join hands with my enemy and thus revenge himself on me. And so I shall hide somewhere so as to find out what he is up to and to make sure that he does not lead my enemy straight here to kill me, for they say:

'A strong man who puts his faith in others,
May pay with his life,
But a weakling who is always wary,
Escapes death,
Even at the hands of the strongest of men.' "

And so having come to this decision, Pingalaka took off and waited anxiously for Damanaka's return.

In the meantime, Damanaka came near to where Sanjivaka was, and realised that it was only a bullock, making the noise. He was overjoyed, thinking to himself, "This is a lucky omen: now I shall have Pingalaka under my thumb because I have the power to make him and this bullock friends or enemies, whichever I choose, for:

'As a man in good health requires no doctor
So a king free from troubles pays no attention to his minister.' "

With these thoughts, Damanaka returned and searched out Pingalaka. Bowing before him, he took his place.

—"So did you see him?" asked Pingalaka.

—"With your good favour I have seen him," replied Damanaka.

—"Honestly?" asked Pingalaka. "Are you telling the truth?"

—"Do you think anyone would dare lie to you?" said Damanaka.

—"So, it's true?" said Pingalaka, "You have seen him. The great do not assert themselves against weaklings, that's why he did not kill you, for:

'The storm spares the low-bowing and weak grass
But uproots the tall trees.
The strong fight the strong
But not the weak.' "

—"Well. however great he may be, and however helpless we seem by comparison," said Damanaka, "just say the word and I will make him your servant!"

Pingalaka breathed a sigh of relief and said, "What! Could you really do that?"

—"What is impossible for a man of intelligence?" replied Damanaka.

—"Well," said Pingalaka, "if that is the case, I appoint you my minister from this very day."

Damanaka took his leave and went straight to Sanjivaka. He began to scold him, "Despicable ox! Aren't you afraid of our master Pingalaka that you bellow at such odd hours? Come with me. My master Pingalaka has summoned you."

When Sanjivaka heard this he said, "My dear fellow, who is this Pingalaka?"

—"What!" exclaimed Damanaka. "You haven't heard of Pingalaka? Just you wait, you'll get to know him alright soon! He is over there, sitting under the banyan tree, surrounded by his retinue."

When Sanjivaka heard this, he thought that his end had come and his heart sank. He said to Damanaka, "My friend, you seem sympathetic and an expert in the arts of conversation. If you want to take me to the lion, get me a guarantee that my life will be safe."

—"You are right to ask for security," said Damanaka, for:

'A man can reach the ends of the earth
Or the depths of the sea
Or the tops of the mountains
But none can fathom the deep thoughts of a king.'

—"So wait here. I shall take you to him when the time is ripe."

Then Damanaka returned to Pingalaka and said, "Master, that is no ordinary animal. He is an ox who is a special mount of Shiva*. When I asked him he explained to me, 'My Lord Shiva was very pleased with me and gave me leave to enjoy the tender grass of the river Yamuna. And Lord Shiva said that the whole jungle should be my playground.' "

—"Now I know the truth!" exclaimed Pingalaka terrified. "How else could a grass-eating animal wander fearlessly in a jungle full of dangerous beasts, except he had the blessings of Shiva. But what did you say to him when you heard that?"

—"Master," said Damanaka, "I told him, 'This jungle has already been presented to our master by the goddess Durga*, whose mount he is. But, all the same, you are welcome. Come and stay with king Pingalaka as if you were his own brother, spend your time making merry with food and drink and games.' Well, he agreed but has requested that you should guarantee that his life will be safe. So, the rest is up to you."

When Pingalaka heard this, he said, "Well done, my efficient minister. You have acted exactly according to my wishes. I do assure him that his life shall be safe but get me a similar assurance from him too and bring him to me quickly."

Damanaka bowed before Pingalaka and, on his way to Sanjivaka, he thought gleefully, "My master is very gracious towards me and is behaving exactly as I hoped. I think I must be the luckiest being alive."

When he reached Sanjivaka, he said to him respectfully, "Friend, I made a request to my master that your life should be spared. He has promised that it shall be so. And so, accompany me with confidence. But when we arrive at the king's place, you should respect me as much as you respect yourself. Don't get too big for your boots and start bossing me about. On my part, I shall

consult you in the exercise of my duties as a minister.
In this way, we can both enjoy Lakshmi*, for:

'A man who, out of pride,
Does not properly handle the high, the middle and
    the low,
Shall be ruined, as Dantila* was ruined,
Even though he was the favourite of the king.' "

—"How was that?" asked Sanjivaka.

And Damanaka told:

THE STORY OF THE MERCHANT DANTILA

"Somewhere in the world, is a city called Vardhamana*.
A very prosperous merchant, by the name Dantila, lived
there. He exercised authority over the whole city. During
his administration, he kept both the common people
and the king very happy. What more can be said? A
man as wise as that has hardly been heard of or seen,
for:

'The man who seeks the good of the king,
Is hated by the common people
And the man who seeks the welfare of the people,
Is hated by the king.'

"In such conflicting circumstances, it is almost
impossible to find such a man, loved by the king as
well as the people.

"In the course of time, the marriage of Dantila's
daughter took place. Dantila invited the entire public
and the king's officers. He entertained them sumptuous-
ly, gave them presents of clothing and in this way, he
honoured them. After the wedding, the king himself
with queen and the entire court were invited along to
Dantila's house and he showed them great respect.

"A servant by the name of Gorambha*, who used to
sweep the floors of the king's palace, came there too,
but uninvited. He sat down on a seat meant for someone
else. Dantila caught him by the neck and threw him
out.

"The servant felt insulted and could not sleep all night
for thinking, 'How can I get Dantila into disfavour with
the king and so get even with him. But then, what
chance have I, an ordinary fellow, of harming such a
powerful person as he is.'

"Several days later, early in the morning, when the
king was not yet wide awake, Gorambha was sweeping
the floor near his bed and said, 'Good heavens! Dantila
has become so brazen nowadays that he actually dares

to embrace the queen!'

"When the king heard this, he jumped up and shouted, 'Gorambha! Is that true? Has Dantila really embraced the queen?'

— 'Master,' replied Gorambha, 'I was gambling all night and didn't sleep at all. This morning I feel drowsy. I really don't know what I've been saying.'

"Jealous, the king thought to himself, 'Yes! The servant Gorambha is allowed to go about freely in the palace and so is Dantila. It is quite possible that Gorambha has seen Dantila embracing my queen, for:

"What a man ponders over, sees or performs
During the day,
He will mutter in his dreams."

— 'And there is no doubt about it when a woman is involved. She smiles at one man, with half-opened lips, throws a little remark at another, at the same time flirting with the third, her eyes half-closed, whilst in her heart she dreams of yet another man, the one she loves. Who can depend on the love of such a woman, with eyebrows like the bows of an archer? The man who thinks that a woman loves him, is a fool. He falls into her trap — she'll treat him like a toy.'

"The king's thoughts were so troubled that, from that day onward, he withdrew his favours from Dantila and, what is more, he forbade him even to enter the palace. Dantila was astounded to see this sudden change in the king's attitude and said to himself, 'It's true what they say:

"Has anyone heard of
A crow that is clean,
A gambler who is honest,
A snake that forgives,
A passionate woman who is calm,
An impotent man who is brave,
A drunkard with discrimination,
Or the friendship of a king."

— 'Even in my dreams, I have done no harm to anyone,

not to the king himself, nor to anyone in his family. Why then is the king so hostile towards me?'

"Some time passed.

"One day, when Dantila wanted to pass through the gateway to the palace, he was stopped by the guards. Gorambha, who was sweeping the floor, saw this and he said with a smirk, 'Ho! Guards! That fellow is the king's favourite. He can arrest or release people, just as he pleases. He threw me out. Be careful, you may suffer the same fate.'

"When Dantila heard this, he thought to himself, 'It is surely Gorambha who has caused the trouble. Now I understand why they say:

"The king's servant,
    Though he be of low caste, foolish or mean,
    Is respected wherever he goes." '

"Dantila felt upset and returned home in a very dejected mood. He thought it over and that evening, he invited Gorambha to his house, gave him a pair of garments and said kindly, 'My dear friend, it was not because I was angry that I threw you out that day but because it was an impropriety for you to take the seat you took — it was reserved for a Brahmin. The Brahmin felt insulted, that's why I had to throw you out. Forgive me.'

"When Gorambha saw the clothes, he was very pleased. Full of joy, he said to Dantila, 'Sir, now I forgive you. You have expressed your regrets and also honoured me. Once again you shall see the favour of the king and in this way I shall prove to you my cleverness.' With these words Gorambha went home happily.

"Next morning, he went to the palace and started sweeping the floor. When he had made sure that the king was lying half-awake, he said, 'The king is really indiscreet, he eats cucumber in the lavatory!'

"The king was taken aback to hear this and he shouted, 'You! Gorambha! What's that nonsense you're talking! It's only because you're my servant that I don't kill you.

Have you ever seen me doing such a thing?'

— 'Master,' said Gorambha, 'I was gambling last night and didn't sleep at all. This morning I feel drowsy. I really don't know what I've been saying. But if I've said anything out of place, please forgive me.'

"When the king heard this, he thought to himself, 'Never in my life have I eaten cucumber in the lavatory. If this fool has said something ridiculous about me, surely what he said about Dantila was ridiculous too. It was wrong of me to have insulted Dantila. Besides, without him, the whole administrative system, at the palace and in the city, has become slack.'

"When he had considered this carefully, the king invited Dantila to the palace, presented him with jewels and clothing and reappointed him to his former position.

—"And so," continued Damanaka, "that's why I said:

'A man who, out of pride,
Does not properly handle the high, the middle and
   the low,
Shall be ruined, as Dantila was ruined,
Even though he was the favourite of the king.' "

—"Brother," said Sanjivaka, "you're right, I'll do exactly as you say."

Then Damanaka brought Sanjivaka to Pingalaka and said, "Master, I have brought Sanjivaka to you. Now I leave everything in your hands."

Sanjivaka bowed before Pingalaka and stood before him respectfully. Pingalaka greeted him with similar respect and asked, "My friend, how is the world with you? How do you come to be in this wild jungle?" And Sanjivaka told him all that had happened to him.

When Pingalaka had finished listening to Sanjivaka's story, he said kindly, "My dear Sanjivaka, don't be afraid. Move about as freely as you please in this jungle, which my claws and arms protect. However, you must always stay near me, for this jungle is inhabited by wild beasts, dangerous even to very powerful animals, to say nothing of grass-eaters."

With this, Pingalaka went to the bank of the river
Yamuna to drink water to his heart's content. And then
he returned to the jungle. He entrusted the administration of the kingdom to Karataka and Damanaka and
began to listen to Sanjivaka's moral tales — this is how
he spent his time.

Sanjivaka had made a thorough study of the shastras*,
and, in a few days, he considerably enlightened the dull
Pingalaka and made him forget his wild mannerisms.

Every day they had discussions together in secret. All
the other animals stayed at a distance, even Damanaka
and Karataka were forbidden to approach them.

As the lion would no longer go hunting, all the animals
including Damanaka and Karataka began to starve. They
say:

> "As birds forsake an old and withered tree,
> No longer bearing fruit and fly elsewhere,
> So servants forsake a king,
> From whom they no longer benefit."

When Karataka and Damanaka had given up all hope
of a change in the king's attitude, they held a discussion
together.

—"Brother Karataka," said Damanaka, "again we're in
a spot. Ever since Pingalaka has been taken up by this
talk of Sanjivaka's, he has neglected all his responsibilities.
His entire court has deserted him. Now what are we
going to do?"

—"Even if the master does not listen to you," said
Karataka, "it is still your duty to set his faults right. It's
a minister's duty to advise a king, whether the king
accepts his advice or not. If a proud king or an agitated
elephant follows the wrong path, it's the fault of the
minister and the *mahout*. You brought the grass-eating
Sanjivaka to the master. You yourself have raked the
burning coals."

—"That's very true," said Damanaka. "It is my fault,
not the master's. They say:

> 'The jackal between the fighting rams

And the Sanyasi* who trusted Ashadhbhuti*,
Were themselves to blame.' "
—"How was that?" asked Karataka.
And Damanaka told:

THE STORY OF THE JACKAL AND THE SANYASI

"Once upon a time, in a lonely matha*, there lived a Sanyasi called Dev Sharma*. Many people used to visit him and present him with finely woven garments, which he sold and got very rich on the proceeds. As a result of being so rich, he trusted nobody. Night and day he kept the treasure purse under his armpit and would not part with it even for a second. As they say:

'Getting money is an arduous toil
And guarding it is even more of a trial.
Coming and going money causes trouble,
Damn this unending source of worry!'

"A swindler by the name of Ashadhbhuti, who robbed other men of their money, noticed that the Sanyasi kept the treasure purse under his armpit. He said to himself, 'How could I rob this man of his money! It's difficult to make a hole through the walls of the matha or to get in over the high gates, so what I'll do is charm him with honeyed words so that he accepts me as his disciple. And when he has put confidence in me, some day he'll fall into my clutches. As they say:

"A man who has no desires,
Doesn't deprive others of their rights."

And,

"A man with no passion
Doesn't adorn himself,
The fool does not speak subtly,
And the man who speaks out his mind,
Is never a cheat." '

"When he had resolutely made up his mind, to carry out this plan, Ashadhbhuti approached Dev Sharma, stood before him with reverence and said, 'Om Namaha Shivaya*!' With these words, he threw himself humbly on the ground before Dev Sharma and said, 'Oh, Bhagawan, this life is futile! Youth gushes by, like a mountain stream. Life is like a fire in the grass, all its

pleasures are as transient as the clouds in autumn, and
one's relationship with friends, sons, wives and servants
is no more than a dream. This I have clearly realised.
Now guide me that I may cross the ocean of life.'

"When Dev Sharma heard this, he said kindly, 'My
son, you are indeed blessed that you have come to give
up the world in your youth. You ask for direction to
cross this ocean of life. Then listen. According to my
way of thinking:

> "The good man's mind
> Has the peace of old age
> Whilst his body is still young,
> But the wicked man's body
> Is feeble with age
> Whilst his mind remains young." '

"When Ashadhbhuti heard this, he fell on the ground
before Dev Sharma, touched his feet, and said, 'Oh,
Bhagawan, initiate me in the secrets!'

— 'My child!' answered Dev Sharma, 'I will, but on one
condition, that you will never enter the matha at night,
because Sanyasis are recommended to stay alone at night
without company, and we will keep to it, you and I.
For they say:

> "A king is ruined through bad advisers,
> A Sanyasi through company,
> A son through over-indulgence,
> A Brahmin through lack of studying the shastras,
> A business or a farm through neglect,
> And a family and character through contact with
>   bad people."

— 'And so,' continued Dev Sharma, 'after taking the
vow of initiation, you will have to sleep in a thatched
hut at the gate of the matha.'

— 'I shall willingly carry out your wishes,' said
Ashadhbhuti.

"At bedtime, Dev Sharma initiated Ashadhbhuti
according to the rituals and made him his disciple.
Ashadhbhuti massaged his hands and feet, waited upon

him and made him happy but nonetheless Dev Sharma did not part with his money bag even for a second.

"After some time, Ashadhbhuti began to think, 'He does not trust me at all! Shall I knife him in broad daylight, poison him or kill him like a wild animal?'

"While he was thinking this over, the son of one of Dev Sharma's disciples, from a nearby village, came to give him a personal invitation and said, 'Bhagawan! Today the ceremony of the sacred thread* takes place in our house. Please come and sanctify it with your presence.'

"Dev Sharma gladly accepted the invitation and Ashadhbhuti accompanied him. On the way, they came to a river. When Dev Sharma saw the river, he folded his money bag in his robe and said, 'Ashadhbhuti, look after this robe with the vigilance of a Yogi* until I return.' And he went into the bushes. The minute Dev Sharma's back was turned, Ashadhbhuti vanished with the money bag.

"Meanwhile, as Dev Sharma was answering the call of nature, he saw in the distance, two golden rams, fighting each other. They rammed into each other until the blood oozed out, but still they refused to stop fighting.

"Meanwhile, a blood-thirsty jackal arrived on the scene and began to lick the blood from the ground. Dev Sharma thought to himself, 'If he comes in between the two fighting rams, he's sure to get himself killed.'

"Sure enough, craving for the blood, the jackal got caught up in the fight. He was hit on the head, fell down and died.

"Dev Sharma finished what he was doing and slowly returned, thinking about this incident and also about his money. When he got back, he failed to find Ashadhbhuti but saw only his robe, lying on the ground. He peered anxiously inside it but could not find his purse. He began to cry out, 'Alas! I have been robbed!' And he fell to the ground, in a swoon.

"After a minute or so, he returned to his senses. He

got up and began to shout 'Ashadhbhuti, where are you, you swindler! Answer me!' After he had shouted like this in a loud voice, he slowly trailed Ashadhbhuti's footsteps until, just before evening, he came to a village. He stayed there a short time and then returned to his matha.

—"And so," continued Damanaka, "that's why I said:

'The jackal between the fighting rams
And the Sanyasi who trusted Ashadhbhuti,
Were themselves to blame.' "

—"So, under the circumstances, what should we do?" said Karataka.

—"At this very moment, I'm getting inspiration," said Damanaka. "I shall cleverly create discord between him and the master and separate them, for they say:

'An arrow, shot from a bow
May or may not kill a man,
But the wit of a clever man
Can destroy a host of enemies.' "

—"Oh, but brother!" said Karataka. "If, somehow or other, Pingalaka or Sanjivaka, finds out about your scheme to bring about discord between them, you're done for!"

—"My dear Karataka," said Damanaka, "don't talk like that. When you fall on bad times and luck's against you, you should go on trying, for:

'Lakshmi bestows her favours,
On the zealous man.
She scorns the idle,
Who depend entirely on luck.
So, brush destiny aside
And try with all your might.
If you still fail,
Find out what went wrong.'

—"And so," Damanaka went on, "that's why I shall continue to work on them so subtly that neither of them will have a chance to know anything about it."

When he heard this, Karataka said, "Very well the..

brother, but I feel frightened because Sanjivaka is wise
and the lion is fierce. Even though you have a sharp
wit, I think it's beyond your power to separate them
and get away with it."

—"It may seem beyond me," said Damanaka, "but I'll
manage it, for:

'What cannot be achieved by force,
Can be achieved through deceit.
With the help of the gold chain,
The female crow killed the black cobra.' "

—"How was that?" asked Karataka.

And Damanaka told:

THE STORY OF THE COBRA AND THE CROW

"Somewhere in the country, under a banyan tree, there lived a pair of crows, husband and wife. Now, whenever the female hatched her eggs, a black cobra would come out of the hollow of the tree, climb up, and make a meal of them.

"Nearby, under another banyan tree, there lived a jackal. The crows told him everything. 'Friend,' they said, 'the black cobra creeps out of the hollow of the tree and eats up our children. Tell us, what can we do to protect them? It's become dangerous for us to live here.'

— 'Don't give up hope,' said the jackal, 'it's a fact that an enemy can be destroyed by a trick. An ordinary fellow, if he's cunning, escapes being overpowered by the strongest of men. A very greedy heron, who was feeding on small, medium and large-sized fishes, was killed by a mere crab!'

— 'How was that?' asked the female crow.

And the jackal told:

THE STORY OF THE HERON AND THE CRAB

" 'Somewhere in the jungle, there was a big lake, and in it lived all kinds of water creatures. A heron also lived there. He had grown old and had no strength left to catch the fishes. Because he was starving, he had become lean.

" 'One day, he came to the edge of the pond and began to cry loudly, shedding his tears like pearls. A crab came up to him (a number of fishes were also with him) and asked sympathetically, "Uncle! Are you alright? Why aren't you eating today and why are you crying? Why these sighs?"

—"Ah, child," replied the heron, "I have decided to renounce the world. I have been a fish-eater but now I wouldn't touch them even if they come near me, for I have undertaken a fast unto death."

—"What is the reason for your renunciation?" the crab asked him.

—"Well," said the heron, "I was born in this pond and it is here I've grown old. Now I have heard that there will be no rain here for the next twelve years."

—"Where have you heard that?" exclaimed the crab.

—"From the mouth of an astrologer," said the heron. "He said that it is written in an astrological book that, due to the planetary positions, there will be no rain for twelve years. There's not much water in this pond now, it will get less and less and in the end, it will dry up completely. Consequently, without water, the water creatures I grew up with and played games with will die. I cannot bear to be separated from them. That's why I've taken on this fast unto death. The water creatures of the small ponds are being evacuated to larger ones by their relatives, while the tortoises, crocodiles and the bigger animals are going elsewhere on their own. But the water creatures here don't seem to care. I am crying because everything will be completely wiped out."

" 'The crab told this to the other water creatures. All the crabs, fishes, tortoises and everybody were in a state of panic. They went to the heron and said, "Is there no way out? Can't we protect ourselves against this disaster?"

—"Well," said the heron, "not far from here is a lake, full of water. Even if there was no rain for twenty-four years, this lake, which is covered with lotus flowers, will never dry up. If somebody rides on my back I can take him there."

" 'And, in this way, he gained their confidence. They gathered round him, crying, "Uncle! Father! Brother! Me first! Me first! Please!" The wicked heron took them, one by one, on his back. When he had flown a little away, he would smash them against a rock and eat them to his heart's content. When he got back, he would deliver false messages to their relatives.

" 'One day the crab said to the heron, "Uncle, I was friends with you first and yet you take the others before me. Now save my life too." When he heard this, the heron thought to himself, "I am tired of eating fish everyday. To change the monotony of the food, I'll eat this crab today." And so he took the crab on his back and carried him to the rock where he had killed the fishes. The crab recognised the heap of bones and the skeletons of the fishes and understood everything. But calmly he said to the heron, "Uncle! Say, how far is this pond? You must be tired of carrying me. I am very heavy." The heron thought to himself, "Now this dumb water creature is in my power, he cannot escape my clutches." So, with a smirk, he said to the crab, "Crab, where could there be another pond? This trip is for my food. I am going to smash you against this rock and eat you."

" 'As soon as the heron had said this, the crab put his claws round the white, lotus-like neck of the heron and strangled him to death.

" 'The crab slowly dragged the neck back to the pond. All the water dwellers gathered round him and began to ask, "Crab, why are you back? And why hasn't uncle returned with you? Why is he wasting time? We are all impatient for a chance to be taken."

" 'Then the crab laughed and said, "You fools! That swindler was not taking the water creatures to any pond; he was smashing them against a rock, not far from here, and eating them. I was destined to stay alive and understood what he was up to. I killed the trickster and I've brought back his neck. Now there's no need to worry. We are safe."

—'That's why I said,' continued the jackal, 'a greedy heron, who was feeding on large, medium and small-sized fishes, was killed by a mere crab.'

"After listening to this, the crow said, 'Friend, tell us how we can kill the wicked cobra.'

—'Well,' said the jackal, 'go to a city that is the capital of a kingdom. Visit the house of some wealthy man, a minister or someone, and see if they have been careless enough to leave a gold chain or a necklace lying about. Pick it up, and making sure that the servants are watching you, fly off slowly with it and drop it in the hollow of the tree where the snake lives. When the servants run after you to get the necklace back, they'll see the snake and it's certain they'll kill him.'

"The crows decided to take the jackal's advice and flew off. As they were flying, the female noticed a lake, in which the women of the harem were swimming. They had left gold and pearl necklaces with their clothes on the bank of the lake. The female crow picked up a gold chain in her beak and started flying slowly to her nest.

"When the eunuchs saw this, they picked up their sticks and started running after the female crow. She let the gold chain fall near the hollow of the tree where the snake lived and seated herself on a tree near by. When the king's servants arrived on the scene, they were confronted by a snake with swelling hood, before

the hollow of the tree. They killed him with sticks,
recovered the gold chain and returned home. And the
crows lived happily ever after.

—"And so," continued Damanaka, "that's why, I said:

'What cannot be achieved by force,
Can be achieved through deceit.'

—"Nothing in this world is impossible for a clever man.
Because he was clever, the hare killed a mighty lion
living in the jungle."

—"How was that?" asked Karataka.

And Damanaka told:

THE STORY OF THE LION AND THE HARE

"In the jungle, there lived a lion by the name of Bhasuraka*. He was very powerful and used to kill the other animals indiscriminately.

"One day, all the antelopes, boars, buffaloes, hares, and the rest went together to the lion and said, 'Master, why do you persist in killing so many of us everyday so unnecessarily, when one animal would satisfy your hunger? Please come to an understanding with us. From today onward we promise to send to your lair, one animal everyday for your food, if in return you guarantee that we shall be able to wander about unmolested in the jungle. In this way, you will have no trouble maintaining yourself and we won't be killed so indiscriminately. They say:

"As by taking medicine in small doses,
A man grows strong,
So too a king becomes powerful
By taxing his subjects bit by bit.
A cow must be well cared for,
Before she yields milk
And the creepers watered
Before they give beautiful flowers,
So too a king must take care of his subjects,
If he wants to get the best out of them." '

"When he had finished listening to this, Bhasuraka said, 'It's very true, what you say, but if I don't receive one animal everyday, I shall eat every one of you!'

"The animals promised that they would keep their word. Accordingly, everyday they drew lots, sent one animal to the lion and roamed in the jungle, unafraid.

"One day it was the hare's turn. Forced by the other animals, he made his way to the lion, slowly and very much against his will.

"On the way, the hare was considering how he might kill the lion, when he came to a well. He leapt up on the edge and saw his reflection in the water. At this, he thought to himself, 'Now I know a way that won't fail. I'll deceive the lion and make him fall into the well.'

"By the time the hare reached the lion, the sun was setting. Bhasuraka was in a fury because he had been kept waiting. He licked his lips hungrily and said to himself, 'The first thing I'll do tomorrow is kill all those animals!'

"When he was thinking this, the hare came slowly and stood before him. The lion flared up and began to shout at him, 'You miserable creature! First you are too small and secondly you are late. Well, for this, I'm going to kill you immediately and I'll kill the rest of them in the jungle tomorrow morning.'

—'Master,' replied the hare very humbly, 'it is not my fault nor the fault of the other animals. Please listen and I will explain.'

—'Hurry up and tell me before I crush you!' said the lion.

—'Well,' said the hare, 'today it fell to my lot to come to you. Because I am small, they sent four other hares with me. On the way, a huge lion came out of the den and cried, "Ho! You! Where are you going? Call upon your chosen deity!" And I said, "Sir, we are all going to our master Bhasuraka at the appointed time to fulfil our promise."

'And he said, "Who is this Bhasuraka? I'm the master of the jungle! You should fulfil your promises only to me. Bhasuraka is an imposter! I shall hold four of you hares as hostages while you (meaning me) go and challenge Bhasuraka to a trial of strength with me. Whoever turns out to be stronger, deserves to be king of the jungle and only he shall eat all the hares!"

—'And so,' continued the hare, 'I have come to you as he ordered me to. That is why I am late. Now, do as you think best.'

"When he heard this, Bhasuraka said, 'Friend, if this

is true, then take me to this pretender immediately so that I can pour out on him all my rage against you and then I shall be quiet!'

—'Master,' said the hare, 'it is the truth, but this lion lives in a stronghold. It's difficult to attack someone who is hiding in a stronghold, for they say:

"A single archer, behind the wall of a castle
Can fight a hundred men of the enemy." '

"When he heard this, Bhasuraka replied, 'Friend! He may have hidden himself in his stronghold, but just show him to me and I'll kill him, for they say:

"Suppress your enemies and diseases
At the very beginning
Or they will become strong
And destroy you." '

—'That's true,' said the hare, 'but I've seen him. He is very strong. It would be unwise of you to approach him without finding out exactly what his strength is, for they say:

"He who attacks an enemy,
Without knowing his strength,
Is sure to be destroyed,
Like a moth in the fire." '

—'That's not your concern,' said Bhasuraka, 'just take me to him!'

—'Very well then,' said the hare, 'come with me.'

"The hare went ahead so as to lead the lion to the well.

'When they reached the well, the hare said to the lion, 'My Lord! Who can withstand your power! The imposter has seen you coming and has hidden himself in his stronghold!' And the hare pointed out the well.

"The foolish lion saw his reflection in the water and imagined that it was his enemy. He roared fearfully and at once his roar was doubly re-echoed from the well. Furious at the other lion, he leapt in upon him and was drowned.

"Very pleased with himself, the hare went back to the

jungle and told the other animals what had happened. They showered him with praise and all lived happily ever after.

—"And so," continued Damanaka, "that's why I said: It's the clever man who is powerful. Now, if you think fit, I shall use my cleverness to create dissension between the lion and Sanjivaka."

—"If you can," said Karataka, "then do it. And may God protect you."

One day, shortly afterwards, seeing Pingalaka sitting apart from Sanjivaka, Damanaka bowed and stood before him.

—"My friend!" said Pingalaka. "Where have you been hiding for so long?"

—"I didn't come," said Damanaka, "because you wouldn't have anything to do with me. But I have come now, of my own accord, to talk with you because I see the impending destruction of all your administration and my heart is heavy with grief."

When he heard Damanaka speaking so intently, Pingalaka asked him, "What are you trying to say to me? Out with it!"

—"Master," replied Damanaka, "Sanjivaka hates you! This very ox that you consider to be your friend, is in reality your enemy. He told me in confidence, 'Damanaka, I have got to know all about Pingalaka's strength and weaknesses. I am going to kill him and become king of the animals. Then I shall appoint you as my minister.' "

When Pingalaka heard this, he was flabbergasted, as if a thunderbolt had struck him, and he could not speak.

Damanaka saw this and thought to himself, "Pingalaka certainly has too much confidence in Sanjivaka. Undoubtedly this will lead to Pingalaka's destruction. They say:

'When a king submits himself entirely
To one adviser,
That man becomes haughty and mad for power:

He will try to be independent
And as this desire grows in his heart,
In the end he will secretly plan the king's death.' "
  After some time, Pingalaka recovered himself and said,
"What shall I do? Sanjivaka has become as dear to me
as my own life. I cannot believe that he could betray
me."
—"Master," replied Damanaka, "being a servant is always
painful. Only the weak, the ones with no initiative,
faithfully serve the king for ever."
—"All the same," said Pingalaka, "still my mind is not
poisoned against him."
—"Your Majesty," said Damanaka, "you are making a
great mistake. And in any case, what particular virtue
do you see in Sanjivaka? He is a fellow without qualities!
And if you think that he is a heavy animal and will
help you kill your enemies, you are mistaken. He is a
mere grass-eater and all your enemies are carnivorous.
And so, the best thing you can do is accuse him of
some offence and kill him."
—"To find fault with someone after openly singing his
praises," said Pingalaka, "will be like breaking an oath.
Besides, I have given my word, as you advised me to,
that he would be safe. How then can I kill him with
my own hands? Sanjivaka is a real friend to me, I have
no reason whatever to be angry with him, for:
       'It is not good to cut down even a poisonous tree,
         If it has been planted by one's own hands.'
And,
       'First it is foolish to love,
       But if love one must,
       That love should be allowed to grow.'
And again,
         'It is shameful to raise someone up
         And afterwards to cause his downfall.'
—"And so, even if Sanjivaka has turned traitor to me,
I shall not lift my hand against him."
—"Your Majesty," replied Damanaka, "to take pity on

an enemy is against the royal code. And if you follow
this non-violent creed, where will the others get meat
from? If they forsake you, you too will die. When you
are in the company of Sanjivaka, you don't even think
of going out hunting, because:
> 'In the company of the wicked,
> The good follow the wrong path,
> And so the wise shun the company of wicked men.'

And,
> 'Refrain from entertaining a man
> Whose character is unknown.
> The bug was at fault
> But instead they killed the flea.' "

—"How was that?" asked Pingalaka.

And Damanaka told:

THE STORY OF THE BUG AND THE FLEA

"In a certain country lived a king who had a very beautifully decorated bedroom. An exquisite white silk sheet covered the bed and in the folds of the sheet, there lived a white flea, by the name of Mandavisarpini*. She used to drink the blood of the king and, in this way, spent her time very happily.

"One day, a bug by the name of Agnimukha* crept into the bedroom. When the flea caught sight of him, she cried, 'Agnimukha! What are you doing here? Get out at once!'

—'Madam,' replied the bug, 'that's not the way to speak to a guest, even if he is a good-for-nothing. A lady householder should hold out her hand even to someone of low caste. She should say, "Welcome! Please take a seat here and make yourself comfortable. You have visited me after many days. Tell me, what is the latest news? You are looking rather thin. Are you well? I am delighted to see you again!—" '

—'And besides,' continued the bug, 'I have drunk all types of blood, but so far I have never had the pleasure of tasting the blood of a king. I think it must be very sweet, for he has been eating the choicest food. Now, if you will permit me, I would love to taste the king's blood. I have come to your house faint with hunger. Mandavisarpini, it is unworthy of you to enjoy the king's blood all to yourself! Let me too have a share of it.'

—'But, Agnimukha,' said the flea, 'I only suck the king's blood when he has gone fast asleep but you are nasty and bite like a sharp needle. However, if you promise to let the king go to sleep before you start biting him, then I will let you drink his blood.'

—'Oh, I do promise!' replied the bug, 'I will even swear to wait until you have sucked his blood before I suck it myself!'

"While they were talking, the king came and lay down

on the bed. The bug's mouth began to water and he took a bite of the king, without waiting for him to fall asleep. They say:

'You cannot change a person's temperament by preaching,
Even boiled water will finally get cold.'

"The bug's bite was like a sharp needle. The king jumped up and cried out to his servants, 'Hey! Something's bitten me! See if there is a bug or a flea in my bed!'

"When the bug heard this, he hid himself in a corner of the bed. When the servants came and searched with sharp eyes, they found a flea lying between the folds of the sheets, and killed her.

—"And so," continued Damanaka, "that's why I said:

'Refrain from entertaining a man
Whose character is unknown.
The bug was at fault
But instead they killed the flea.'

And they also say:

'He who sacks his own confidants
And engages outsiders in their place,
Shall die like King Kukudruma*.' "

—"How was that ?" asked Pingalaka.

And Damanaka told:

THE STORY OF THE JACKAL WHO FELL INTO A VAT OF INDIGO DYE

"In a jungle, there lived a jackal by the name of Chandarava*. One day he was very hungry, so he went into the city to find food.

"There, he was surrounded by dogs barking loudly. They set upon him and wounded him with their sharp teeth. To save his skin, he ran into a dyer's house. A big vat of indigo dye was lying there. In he jumped and consequently his whole body was dyed indigo — he no longer looked like a jackal.

"When he came out, the dogs were unable to recognize him and ran off in all directions, terrified.

"The jackal himself went back to the jungle. The indigo dye would not come off. As they say:

'Glue, an idiot, a woman, a crab,
A shark, indigo dye and a drunkard,
Once they attach themselves to something,
They will never let go.'

"Back in the jungle, when the animals, the lions, tigers, elephants, wolves and the rest of them, saw the indigo-coloured jackal, they ran away in terror and said to one another, 'Let's run away for we don't know the strength of this animal or what to expect of him, for they say:

"A man of intelligence who seeks his welfare,
Will never trust anyone
Whose character, family and strength
He does not know." '

"When the jackal saw the frightened animals, he called them back and said, 'Ho! Animals! Why are you running off in panic? Don't be afraid. Brahma* has made me himself, with his own hands, and he said, "The animals have no king, so I have crowned you king, with the title, Kukudruma. Go to the earth and protect them well."

—'And so,' continued the jackal, 'that's why I've come here. Live in my kingdom, under my protection. I, Kukudruma, have been crowned King of the Three Worlds*!'

"When all the animals, the lions, tigers, and the rest of them, heard this, they surrounded him and said, 'Master, we await your commands.'

'Kukudruma assigned specific duties to all the animals, but he said, he would have nothing to do with jackals, and they were all chased away.

"The lion and the tiger used to go out hunting and bring the prey before the jackal. He would then distribute it amongst the other animals. Thus, he discharged his kingly duties.

"In this way, quite some time elapsed. One day, Kukudruma heard in the distance the howl of a pack of jackals. He was spellbound, his eyes filled with tears of joy, he stood up and began to howl.

"When the lion and the other animals heard him howl, they realised that he was only a jackal and they lowered their heads in shame.

"Only for a moment did they remain in this attitude. Then they said angrily to each other, 'This despicable jackal has fooled us! We will kill him!'

"When Kukudruma heard this, he tried to escape but was torn in pieces on the spot and killed.

—"And so," continued Damanaka, "that's why I said:

'He who sacks his own confidants
    And engages outsiders in their place,
    Shall die like King Kukudruma.' "

When he heard this, Pingalaka asked, "But, what proof do you have in this case, that Sanjivaka has evil designs against me?"

—"Here is the proof," said Damanaka. "This morning he made a firm resolution in front of me to kill you. Now, tomorrow morning, when he visits you, his eyes will be red, his lips quivering and he will give you a

malicious look. When you see this, do what you think
best."

Then Damanaka came to Sanjivaka, bowed and stood
humbly before him

When Sanjivaka saw Damanaka, he said, "Worthy
friend, welcome! You have visited me after many days.
Are you well? Tell me what your wishes are and I shall
certainly fulfil them."

—"How can servants be well?" replied Damanaka. "They
say:

'The poor, the sick, fools, exiles,

And servants who have to serve all their lives,

All these, although living,

Are, in reality, dead.'

—"To say that service is dog's work is untrue, for even
dogs are allowed to wander wherever they please, but
servants cannot even leave the house without their
master's permission."

—"Come to the point," said Sanjivaka. "What are you
trying to say?"

—"Friend," replied Damanaka, "it's wrong for a minister
to expose his master's secrets, but still, I will, in order
to save your life. For I know that you trust me implicitly
and it was on my advice that you first came to this
place. Now understand this: Pingalaka has evil designs
against you! Today he said to me in confidence,
'Tomorrow I shall kill Sanjivaka, invite all the animals
to a feast and feed them on his flesh.' I said to him,
'Master! It is shameful to betray a friend in order to
fill one's own belly!' Immediately he said to me, 'You
fool! Sanjivaka is a grass-eater and we flesh-eaters. We
are natural enemies. If we kill him, we are not at fault.'
When I understood that Pingalaka was resolute, I came
to you so that I shall not be guilty of betraying someone
who trusts me. That's why I have confided everything
in you. Now do whatever you think best."

When Sanjivaka heard these words, he was

dumbfounded, as if struck by a thunderbolt. When he had recovered a little, he sighed deeply and said to himself,

"The fool who thinks that a king loves him,
Should be thought of as an ox without horns."

—"It was wrong of me to make friends with Pingalaka, for:

'Enter into marriage ties and friendship
Only with those, who are socially and financially
Your equals.'

—"And so, even if I try to appease Pingalaka, it will be completely pointless, for:

'If a man is angry for some reason,
He calms down,
When the cause is removed.
But who can appease a man
Who decides upon enmity
For no reason at all?'

—"I now understand that Pingalaka has been incited against me by people who are jealous of me. This is why he talks as he does when it is quite untrue that I have evil designs against him, for:

'When a man has two wives,
One cannot tolerate
That the other should be preferred.
So the servants of the king
Cannot bear it
When the master favours one of them.' "

—"Friend," said Damanaka, "you shouldn't be afraid. Even if some wicked fellow has made the master angry with you, he will nonetheless be appeased by your charming conversation."

—"My dear fellow," said Sanjivaka, "that's not true. It is impossible to live amongst wicked people, even insignificant ones, for they say:

'Wicked people, although they may be insignificant,
Are mean-minded and live deceptively;

One way or another, they will cause you death,
     Just as the jackal and the others did to the camel.' "
—"How was that?" asked Damanaka.
And Sanjivaka told:

THE STORY OF THE LION, THE CAMEL, THE JACKAL AND THE CROW

"In a certain part of the jungle, there lived a lion king, by the name of Madotkata*. His retinue was comprised of a jackal, a crow and other animals. One day as they were wandering through the jungle, they saw a camel which had been separated from its caravan.
—'This seems to be an extraordinary animal,' said the lion, 'go and ask him where he comes from.'

"The crow spoke up and said, 'Master, this animal is a camel and lives in a village. He is good to eat, so kill him.'

—'I won't kill a guest,' replied the lion. 'Assure him that his life will be spared and bring him to me. Then I can ask him why he is here.'

"They all went to the camel and won his confidence, after assuring him that his life would be safe and brought him to Madotkata.

"The camel bowed and stood before the lion. Madotkata asked him for his story and he told the lion how he had come to be separated from his caravan. When he had finished, the lion said, 'Krathanaka*! Don't return to the village to be a beast of burden. Stay with me. You can live in this jungle without any anxiety and feast on the emerald-coloured grass.' The camel agreed and began to live happily amongst them.

"One day, Madotkata had a fight with a mad elephant and he was wounded by the elephant's sharp tusks, but despite his injuries, he did not die. However, his body became so weak, that he could not take so much as a few steps, and as a result, the crow and all the other animals, dependent on him for food, began to starve.

"Then the lion said, 'Go and find some animal that I can kill even in this condition, so that I can provide food for you.'

"All the animals wandered around everywhere, but

could not find such an animal. Then the crow and the jackal put their heads together.

—'Crow!' said the jackal. 'What's the point of wandering about when this camel could easily be killed to provide us with food?'

—'You're right,' replied the crow, 'but the master has assured him that his life will be spared, so perhaps he won't agree to kill him.'

"Said the jackal, 'I'll influence the master in such a way, that he will agree to kill the camel. Now it's better if you wait here until I come back!'

"With this, the jackal went to the lion and said, 'Master! We have wandered all over the jungle, but have been unable to find any animal at all. What are we to do? We're so starved that we can't even walk properly. But if you were to kill this camel here, his flesh would satisfy all our hunger.'

"When the lion heard his wicked words, he cried out furiously, 'Shame on you, you rascal! Say that again and I will kill you on the spot! How can I kill him, when I've assured him that his life will be safe!'

—'Master!' said the jackal. 'It is certainly a sin to kill him after giving him this guarantee, but if he offers himself to you, of his own free will, then it is no sin to kill him. Otherwise, kill one of us, for you are desperately in need of food to stay alive. What is the good of our lives, if we cannot use them in our master's service. As they say:

"The head of the family

Must be protected in every way possible,

For if he dies, the whole family will come to grief."

—'In any case, if something unfortunate should happen to you, we must all go into the fire and burn ourselves to death.'

"When the lion heard this, he said, 'Then do what you think best.'

"So, the jackal returned to the other animals and said, 'Our master is very sick and who will protect us, if something happens to him? Now nothing is to be gained by wandering around, looking for food, so let us go and offer him our own bodies. In this way, we shall repay our debt to the master.'

"Then they all went and stood before the lion with tears in their eyes and bowed before him.

"When the lion saw them, he asked, 'Well, have you found any animal?' One of them, the crow, said, 'Master, we have wandered everywhere but unfortunately we have not found any such animal. So eat me so that you can stay alive, and for this sacrifice, I shall go to heaven.'

"When the jackal heard this, he said to the crow, 'Your body is too small. Even if the master eats you, it won't keep him alive. Still, you have shown your devotion to him and freed yourself from your debts. You will be praised here on earth and also in heaven. Now I too shall offer myself.'

"Then the jackal stood humbly before the lion and said, 'Master, eat me so that you can stay alive, and for this sacrifice, I shall go to heaven.' But the lion shook his head sadly.

"When the camel saw all this, he thought to himself, 'These two have spoken beautifully, but the master has eaten neither of them, so I too shall take my turn.'

"So the camel said to the jackal and to the crow, 'You have both spoken well, but you are both carnivorous animals and belong to the same caste as the lion, so how can he eat you? Stand aside, I too shall offer myself to him!'

"When the camel had said this, he went and stood before the lion. He bowed low and said, 'Master, you should not kill either of these animals, instead eat me, so that you can stay alive, and for this sacrifice, I shall go to heaven.'

"As soon as the camel had finished speaking, the lion fell on him and tore him apart. And he was eaten by the hungry animals.

—"And so," continued Sanjivaka, "that's why I said:

'Wicked people, although they may be insignificant,
Are mean-minded and live deceptively;
One way or another, they will cause you death,
Just as the jackal and the others did to the camel.'
—"My friend," Sanjivaka went on, "the lion is
surrounded by despicable people. I have thoroughly
understood that. And there is no doubt about it, someone
has aroused his angei against me, that's why he speaks
as he does, for:
'Even soft water drops,
Falling persistently on a rock,
Wear it away:
So too, continuous complaints
Against someone else,
Poison a man's mind.'
—"Ah, well," went on Sanjivaka, "tell me as a friend,
as things stand, what should I do?"
—"Better leave the country and go somewhere else,"
replied Damanaka. 'You should never serve someone
like that, for they say:
'Abandon a master,
Who is conceited
Or unable to differentiate between good and bad,
Or immoral in his way.' "
—"That is true," said Sanjivaka, "but even if I go
somewhere else, I am not sure that I would escape, for
the master is very angry with me and will pursue me
wherever I go. And so, I think that there is no other
honourable alternative for me but to fight him."
When Damanaka heard this, he began to think, "This
cursed ox seems to have made up his mind to fight. If
he were to run his horns through the master, it would
be a disaster for us all. So I must influence him in such
a way that he leaves this place."
Then, aloud, he said to Sanjivaka, "Friend, what you
say is true but is a fight between servant and master
becoming? And what is more:
'He who attacks an enemy

Without knowing his strength,
Will be defeated,
As the Sea was defeated by the tittibha* birds.' "
—"How was that?" asked Sanjivaka.
And Damanaka told:

THE STORY OF THE TITTIBHA BIRDS AND
THE SEA

"Somewhere in the world, on a seashore, there lived a pair of tittibha birds, husband and wife. In the course of time, the female was expecting a family. As the time to lay her eggs came near, she said to her husband, 'My dear, it's almost time for me to lay my eggs. Look for some good safe place, where I can lay them.'

—'Dearest,' said the male tittibha, 'this coast is very nice. You can lay the eggs here.'

—'But,' said she, 'on nights when the moon is full, the Sea here sends its waves so high that they can drag off even a wild elephant. No, find some better place, away from here.'

"When the male tittibha heard this, he laughed and said, 'What a thing to say! The Sea wouldn't dare harm my children! Lay your eggs here and stop worrying!'

"Now, the Sea heard this and thought to himself, 'What kind of impudence is this, from a bird, the size of a worm! For fun, I'll take away his eggs and see what he does.'

"In the course of time, the female laid her eggs. One day shortly afterwards, when the two birds had flown off in search of food, the waves of the Sea came higher and higher and swallowed up the eggs.

"When the birds returned, the female went to her nest and found it empty. She wept bitterly and said to her husband, 'You fool! The waves of the Sea have swallowed my eggs. I asked you to find somewhere else for me to lay them, but you, stupid thing that you are, wouldn't listen to me! They say:

"Those who refuse to follow
The advice of friends who wish them well,
Come to grief,
Like the foolish turtle who fell off the stick.' "

—'How was that?' asked the male tittibha.

And his wife told him:

THE STORY OF THE TURTLE WHO FELL OFF THE STICK

" 'In a certain lake, there lived a turtle, by the name of Kambugriva*. Two swans, whose names were Sankata* and Vikata*, were her friends. Every day, the three of them would go to the bank of the lake and tell each other stories about holy saints and hermits, and then go home at sunset.

" 'After a few years, that part of the country had no rain and, bit by bit, the lake began to dry up.

" 'The two swans were worried about it and said to the turtle, "This lake is becoming nothing but mud. We are worried as to how we will be able to survive here without water."

—"My friends," replied the turtle, "it's quite true that it's impossible to stay here. But we will find some way out, for:

'Even in bad times,
A man should not lose hope,
For by making an effort,
He can certainly find a solution.'

—"So," continued the turtle, "first look for a lake full of water. Then find a strong stick or a rope from somewhere. I shall hold on tight with my mouth to the middle of the stick and you can hold the ends and carry me like this, to the lake."

—"Friend," replied the swans, "we'll do what you suggest, but while we're flying, you mustn't open your mouth to speak, or you will fall off the stick!"

" 'They carried out this plan. When they had flown some distance, the turtle saw below, a town. The town people looked up and saw something being carried in the sky. They said to each other, full of admiration, "Look at that! Those birds are carrying a round thing!"

" 'When the turtle heard the commotion, she opened her mouth to ask, "What's all that noise about!" But of

course the minute she opened her mouth to speak, she
fell down to the earth. And the people hacked her to
pieces and ate her.

—'And so,' continued the female tittibha, 'that's why I
said:

>"Those who refuse to follow
>The advice of friends who wish them well,
>Come to grief,
>Like the foolish turtle who fell off the stick."

And,

>"He who puts his mind to a problem
>Before it presents itself,
>And he who puts his mind to it
>When it actually arrives,
>Both these categories escape,
>But those who depend on luck,
>Will be destroyed,
>As Yadbhavishya* was, by the fishermen." '

—'How was that?' asked the male tittibha.
And his wife told him:

THE STORY OF THE THREE FISHES

" 'In a certain pond, there lived three fishes, their names were: Anagatavidhata*, Pratyutpannamati* and Yadbhavishya*.

" 'One day, some fishermen were passing by. They saw this pond and said to each other, "We have never investigated this particular pond. It's full of fishes! But we already have a good catch today, and it's evening, so let's go home and come back here tomorrow." So the fishermen left.

" 'Now, when Anagatavidhata heard this, he was dumbfounded, as if struck by a thunderbolt, and he called all the fishes together and said to them, "Did you hear what the fishermen said just now? Let's leave immediately for some other pond, for:

'When a weak man meets a stronger opponent,
The best thing he can do is run,
Or else make for a hideout,
There's no other way out.'

—"I think the fishermen will return tomorrow morning," Anagatavidhata went on, "and then they will start killing all the fishes. So it's not wise to stay here a moment longer, for:

'Those who, in time of calamity,
Can without difficulty go elsewhere,
Avoid seeing the destruction,
Of their families and land.' "

" 'When Pratyutpannamati heard this, he said, "You're right! Let us go somewhere else!"

" 'But Yadbhavishya laughed loudly and said, "Oh, I don't agree with you! Would it be right to give up this pond, that belonged to our forefathers, just because of the talk of fishermen! And in any case, if it's time for us to die, death will certainly not spare us, wherever we are, for:

'A man whom fortune smiles on,

Though unprotected, eludes destruction,
But the man with luck against him, is done for,
Even though he be well protected.'
—"So, I won't come with you," continued Yadbhavishya.
"Do as you think best."

" 'When Anagatavidhata heard his decision, he left the
lake immediately with his family.

" 'Early next morning, Pratyutpannamati saw the
fishermen coming in the distance and he too left the
lake with his family.

" 'The fishermen arrived at the lake, threw their nets
and caught all the fishes, including Yadbhavishya and
they all died.

—'And so,' continued the female tittibha, 'that's why I
said:

"He who puts his mind to a problem
Before it presents itself,
And he who puts his mind to it
When it actually arrives,
Both these categories will escape,
But those who depend on luck,
Will be destroyed,
As Yadbhavishya was, by the fishermen." '

—'But my dear,' said the male tittibha, 'do you think
I'm as stupid as Yadbhavishya! You'll see how brilliant
I am when I dry up the Sea!'

—'How can you oppose the Sea!' retorted the female
tittibha, for they say:

"When a weakling gets angry,
He hurts only himself."

And,

"He who attacks an enemy
Without knowing his strength,
Will be destroyed like the moth in fire." '

—'But my dear,' said the male tittibha, 'don't talk like
that! Even when you are small, if you are zealous, you
can overcome even the strongest opponents. As they
say:

"An elephant can be brought under control by a
   goad,
Well, is a goad as big as an elephant?
When a lamp is lighted, the darkness disappears,
Well, is the lamp as big as the darkness?
When a thunderbolt strikes it, the mountain
   crumbles,
Well, is a thunderbolt as big as the mountain?
So the man with zeal is the man who is strong,
The size is unimportant."
—'And so,' continued the male tittibha bird, 'I shall dry
up the whole Sea, by sucking it up in my beak.'
—'My dear fellow,' said his wife, 'how could you suck
up the Sea when the Sindhu* and the Ganga* along
with hundreds of other rivers flow into it. What's the
good of babbling?'
—'My dear,' said the male tittibha, 'my beak is as solid
as iron. Why can't I suck up the Sea, if I work day
and night at it? And until a man puts some effort into
what he is doing, he does not succeed.'
—'My dear,' said the female, 'if you really want to
quarrel with the Sea, then send a message to some of
the other birds and do this with their help, for:
   "Small insignificant things united,
   Become unconquerable;
   Thin blades of grass, woven into a thick rope
   Can tie up an elephant.
   In the same way working together,
   A sparrow, a woodpecker, a fly and a frog
   Killed an elephant." '
—'How was that ?' asked the male tittibha.
And his wife told him:

THE STORY OF THE ELEPHANT
AND THE SPARROW

" 'Somewhere in the jungle, a pair of sparrows had made their nest in a Tamal* tree. In due course, the female sparrow laid her eggs there.

" 'One day, because of tremendous heat, an agitated elephant came and stood under the shade of the tree. With his trunk, he caught hold of the branches supporting the sparrows' nest and pulled them down. The nest fell to the ground and the eggs were smashed. Luckily the sparrows managed to escape but, because she had lost her eggs, the female sparrow was heart-broken and began to cry loudly.

" 'A woodpecker, listening to her sobs, felt touched. He went over to her and said, "My good sparrow, what's the point of crying about it, for they say:

'Wise men don't grieve
Over lost things, the dead
And what belongs to the past:
But a fool weeps over things
Not worth his tears.
He adds sorrow
To the sorrow already existing,
So his suffering is doubled.
That's the difference
Between wise men and fools.' "

—"That's true," said the sparrow, "but this elephant has killed my children. If you are my friend, please find some way of destroying him, so that I can forget the loss of my eggs."

—"I will," said the woodpecker, for:

'A friend is a friend when he helps you in trouble,
A son is a son when he obeys his parents,
A servant is a servant when he performs his duties,
And a wife is a wife when she makes her husband happy.'

And,

    'In affluent times,
    All men are your friends,
    But the person who helps you
    When times are bad,
    Regard him as your true friend,
    Even when he belongs to a different caste.'

—"Now I too have a friend, a fly called Veenarava*. Let's go and ask her to help us, destroy this cruel elephant."

" 'And so, the woodpecker went with the female sparrow to the fly, and said to her, "My friend, this sparrow is a dear friend of mine. A wicked elephant has destroyed her eggs, please help us find a way to kill him."

—"Certainly I'll help you, my good friend," replied the fly, "otherwise, what is a friend for? Now I too have a friend, a frog by the name of Meghanad*. Let's go and ask him to help us destroy this cruel elephant."

" 'And so, they all went together to the frog and told him what had happened. Then the frog said, "What can this elephant do against us, if we work together? Listen, I have a plan. Fly! When the sun is at the highest point, you go and buzz in his ears, so that in sheer ecstasy, he closes his eyes. Then, woodpecker! You peck his eyes, and blind him. Then I will sit at the edge of the pit that's near by and croak. When the elephant is thirsty, hearing me croak, he will come to the pit, thinking it is a lake full of water. He will fall right in and, being unable to get out again, he'll die. Now, if we follow this plan we'll have our revenge."

" 'The others agreed and they carried out the plan successfully: the elephant groped his way to the muddy pit, fell in and died.

—'And so,' continued the female tittibha, 'that's why I said:

    "Working together,

The sparrow, the woodpecker, the fly and the frog,
Killed an elephant." '

—'All right then,' said the male tittibha, 'I'll dry up the
Sea with the help of my friends!'

"And so, the male tittibha sent a call to the crane, the
swan, the peacock and the rest of them, and said, 'The
Sea has insulted us by stealing our eggs. Think of a
way to dry him up completely.'

"At this, all the birds came together to discuss the
situation. 'We can't suck up the Sea in our beaks,' they
said, 'so what's the good of trying? As they say:

"When a weak man, blown up with self-importance,
Attacks a strong enemy,
He has to retreat,
Like an elephant with a broken tusk."

—'Instead, we should go and tell everything to Garuda*,
our king. If he is angry that his people have been
insulted, then he himself will take revenge. But, even
supposing, that out of pride, he refuses to help us, all
the same, we shall feel relieved, for they say:

"When a man can tell his sorrows
To an affectionate friend
Or a dutiful servant,
An obedient wife
Or a powerful master,
That man finds relief."

—'So, we'll all go to Garuda, our master.'

"The birds went to him, with glum faces and tears in
their eyes, and began to sigh piteously, 'Oh Master, what
a catastrophe! You are our protector and yet the Sea
has robbed the good tittibhas of their eggs. If this sort
of thing continues, one day our whole race will be
destroyed. They say:

"A king is a kinsman to those without family,
An eye to the blind,
And a father to the law-abiding.
Just as a gardener looks after his plants,
So a king should take care of his subjects." '

"When Garuda heard the birds wailing, he thought to himself, 'These birds are right! I will go and dry up the Sea!'

"But just as he was thinking this, a messenger arrived from Lord Vishnu*, and said, 'Noble Garuda! I have been sent by Lord Vishnu. He wants you for some divine work in Amaravati*. You had better come quickly with me.'

"When Garuda heard this, he said petulantly, 'Messenger! What could Lord Vishnu want with such a commonplace servant as I am! Please give him my regards and ask him to find another servant instead of me!'

—'Garuda!' said the messenger, 'You've never talked like that before! Tell me, how has our Master offended you?'

—'Well,' said Garuda, 'the Sea, Lord Vishnu'a resting place, has swallowed up the tittibha birds' eggs. If my Lord Vishnu does not force the Sea to return them, I refuse to serve him any more. This is my firm resolution. Go and report all this to your Master.'

"When Lord Vishnu heard from the Messenger that Garuda was sulking, he thought to himself, 'I understand why he is sulking. I'll go and see him myself and pacify him, for they say:

"He who has his own interests at heart,
    Should avoid offending anyone,
    But should handle other with affection,
    As he would his own son." '

"With these thoughts in his mind, Lord Vishnu went quickly to Rukmapur*, where Garuda was.

"When Garuda saw his master coming to his house, he bowed his head with embarrassment and said, 'Master! The Sea, your resting place, by swallowing up the eggs of my servant, has insulted me, but I have restrained myself from punishing him, because of my respect for you, for:

"If you fear the master,
   You don't beat the dog." '

"When Lord Vishnu heard this, he said, 'You're quite right, Garuda. Come with me and we shall take the eggs from the Sea and hand them over to the tittibha birds. Then we'll go to Amaravati.'

"When Lord Vishnu had finished speaking, he reprimanded the Sea and, taking a thunderbolt in his hand, he said, 'Wicked Sea! Return the tittibha birds' eggs at once or I shall dry you up!'

"At this, the Sea was terrified and handed over the eggs to the male tittibha who gave them to his wife.

—"And so," continued Damanaka, "that's why I said:

'He who attacks an enemy
   Without knowing his strength,
   Will be defeated,
   As the Sea was defeated by the tittibha birds."

When Sanjivaka heard this, he asked Damanaka once again, "Friend, how can I know for certain that Pingalaka has evil designs against me, when until now he has always looked on me with increasing favour and I have never before seen any change in his attitude?"

—"Brother!" said Damanaka. "Here is your proof. When you next visit Pingalaka, you will see him with red eyes and vicious looks, rolling his tongue backwards and forward across his lips. Then you will know for sure that he has wicked thoughts. Otherwise, if you see him relaxed and quiet, you will know that he is pleased with you. Now, excuse me, I am going home. Be careful to keep our conversation secret. But if you can leave this very evening and go somewhere else, I advise you to do so. It is much better to leave the country than to stay and fight such a strong enemy."

When Damanaka had left Sanjivaka, he went to see Karataka. When his brother saw him, he said, "Damanaka, what have you been up to?"

—"I have been working hard, sowing the seed of discord between those two," said Damanaka. "Whatever happens

now is the will of Fate. They say:
'Lakshmi bestows her favours,
On the zealous man.
She scorns the idle,
Who depend entirely on luck.
So, brush destiny aside
And try with all your might.
If you still fail,
Find out what went wrong.' "
—"How have you sown the seed of discord?" asked
Karataka.
—"I have made them quarrel by telling each of them
contradictory lies," said Damanaka. "You will never again
see them sitting together, discussing things."
—"It was wrong of you to have separated the two
friends," said Karataka, "for it is far easier to destroy
something than to build it up. As they say:
'The wind has the strength to pull down a tree
But not to raise it again.
So also, a small-minded man can destroy others'
work
But he cannot reconstruct it.' "
—"You don't know anything about the nitishastras," said
Damanaka, "or you would never talk like that, for they
say:
'Suppress your enemy and diseases
At the very beginning,
Or they will become strong
And destroy you.'
—"Sanjivaka has become our enemy. It is because of
him that we have ceased to function as ministers. And
so I have secretly planned his death. But even if he is
not killed, he will certainly run away. You are the only
person to know about this. It's very essential for us to
carry out this plan, to serve our own ends, for:
'Let your heart be hard as stone
And your tongue as soft as butter,
Destroy your enemy without mercy.'

—"With Sanjivaka's death, we derive three benefits. First, we have our revenge; second, we get back our positions as ministers; and third, we shall get his flesh for food. And so how can you find fault with me when his death is so beneficial to us? You know, they say:

'A cunning man,
Even at the cost of tormenting others,
Artfully looks after his own interests
And keeps his plans a secret,
As Chaturaka* the jackal did
In the jungle.' "

—"How was that?" asked Karataka.

And Damanaka told·

THE STORY OF VAJRADAUNSTRA THE LION AND CHATURAKA THE JACKAL

"In a jungle, there lived a lion by the name of Vajradaunstra*. A jackal called Chaturaka and a wolf called Kravyamukha* were his attendants.

"One day, an expectant female camel, who was in labour pains, was left behind by a caravan. In the deep jungle, she fell a prey to the lion. When he had torn off her womb, a little baby camel came out. The lion and the other animals fed themselves on the female camel's flesh and were all very content. But the lion spared the young camel and brought him home alive. He said to him, 'Little camel, you have nothing to fear, either from me or from anyone else, so run about fearlessly in the jungle, just as you please. We'll call you Shankukarana*, because your ears are like wedges.'

"And so the four of them began to live together very happily. They entertained one another telling stories.

"Shankukarana began to grow up but he would never leave the lion even for a moment.

"One day, the lion had a fight with a wild elephant. The elephant wounded the lion so badly with his tusks that Vajradaunstra was unable even to walk. Exhausted with hunger, he said to the others, 'Look for some animal that I can kill, even in this condition, so that your hunger and mine can be satisfied.'

"And so the jackal, the wolf, and the camel, wandered in the jungle until evening, but they could not find any animal at all. So they returned empty-handed.

"Chaturaka the jackal began to think, 'If the lion would only kill Shankukarana, then we could all feed on him for a couple of days. But our master will not kill him, because he has given him the assurance that his life will be safe. However, with the help of my wits, I shall influence the camel in such a way that he will offer himself, of his own accord, to the lion, for:

"There is nothing in this world
That a clever man can't achieve.
So a wise man
Should make the most of his wits." '

"With this thought Chaturaka approached the camel and said to him, 'Shankukarana! The Master is dying of hunger. If he does die, we too shall be destroyed. So I am going to tell you how you could be useful to him. Please listen carefully.'

—'Do tell me,' said Shankukarana, 'and I shall attend to it quickly. And if I do anything for the master, according to our religion, I shall be rewarded a hundred-fold.'

—'Then friend,' said the jackal, 'you should offer your body to the master to save his life, and for this sacrifice, the master will guarantee that you will be given a body, twice your present size, in your next life.'

—'Very well then,' replied Shankukarana, 'I agree.'

"Then all the animals went to the lion and said, 'Master! The sun has already gone down and we have still not been able to find any animal. But if you will guarantee that Shankukarana will have a body twice his present size in the next life, then he is prepared to offer himself to you as a holy sacrifice.'

—'Indeed, I do promise that it shall be so,' replied the lion.

"Hardly had he uttered these words when the wolf and the jackal fell upon the camel and tore up his body. And that was the end of him.

"Afterwards, the lion said to the jackal, 'Chaturaka! Watch this carcass carefully while I go to the river for a bath and worship the gods.' Then the lion went off.

"When he had gone, the jackal thought to himself, 'How can I contrive to enjoy this carcass all to myself?'

"He thought about it for a little while, then he hit upon a plan.

"He said to the wolf, 'Ho! Wolf! You're hungry, aren't you? Until the master comes back, have a few mouthfuls of this camel's flesh. I'll make up a story to tell him, as an excuse, when he returns.'

"But the wolf had hardly begun to eat, when the jackal shouted, 'Look out, Kravyamukha! Here's the master coming back! Leave it alone! Get away from it!' The wolf immediately stopped eating.

"When the lion arrived, he saw that the camel's heart had been removed. He frowned and said angrily, 'Who has contaminated my food? Tell me his name and I shall kill him on the spot!'

"The wolf started looking at the jackal, as much as to say, 'Well, go on, say something to calm him down.'

"But the jackal only smiled and said to the wolf, 'You ate the heart when I told you not to. Now enjoy the fruit of what you have done.'

"When the wolf heard this, he was afraid for his life and took to his heels.

"At this point, a caravan, heavily loaded, was coming along the same path. The leading camel had a large bell round his neck. When the lion heard the jingling sound in the distance, he said to the jackal, 'Go and see where this terrifying noise is coming from. I've never heard it before.'

"The jackal went a little way off, then returned and said, 'Master! Leave this place as quickly as you can, if you want to stay alive!'

—'Friend,' said the lion, 'why are you frightening me? Tell me, what is it?'

—'Master,' said the jackal, 'Yama* is very angry with you, because you have killed a camel before the hour appointed for his death. He has come personally and has brought with him the father and grandfather of the dead camel, to have revenge on you, and the noise you hear, comes from the bell that he has tied round the leading camel's neck.'

"When the lion saw the caravan approaching, he left off eating the camel and ran for his life.

"After that, the jackal had the camel's flesh all to

himself and it lasted him many, many days.

—"And so," continued Damanaka, "that's why I said:

'A cunning man,
Even at the cost of tormenting others,
Artfully looks after his own interests
And keeps his plans a secret,
As Chaturaka the jackal did
In the jungle.' "

After Damanaka had left, Sanjivaka started thinking, "I'm a grass-eater, but I have become the follower of a flesh-eater. I'm in a spot. What shall I do? Where shall I go? How can I get back my peace of mind? Perhaps if I go to Pingalaka and humbly beg for my life, he may not kill me. Then again, suppose I leave this place and go somewhere else . . . ? But no, then some other flesh-eater will kill me. I think it is better to go to the lion."

And so, having made this resolution, Sanjivaka went slowly to the lion's den. He found Pingalaka sitting in exactly the same attitude as Damanaka had described. So shocked was Sanjivaka that he immediately backed away from the lion and stood, at a distance, without even bowing to him. And so it was that Pingalaka too saw Sanjivaka in the same attitude as Damanaka had described.

Furiously, he fell upon the bullock, tearing his back with his sharp claws. Sanjivaka pointed out his horns against Pingalaka's belly and stood, ready to fight.

When Karataka and Damanaka saw the lion and the bullock thus confronting each other, with faces red as the Kinshuka* flower and eyes like fire, Karataka said to his brother, "You stupid fellow! You did wrong in creating enmity between these two. This proves that you don't really know the nitishastras, for they say:

'Only a man who can reach his goal
Through cunningness and intrigue,
Avoiding war,
Deserves to be a minister.'

—"So if you are really shrewd, you must now find a way to bring this conflict to an end. Otherwise, both of them will be destroyed. On the other hand, if only the bullock is killed and you regain your position as minister, then everyone will avoid the master. As they say:

'A good king, served by a wicked minister,
Is shunned by all,
Just like a lake of sweet water,
When it has crocodiles all round it.'

—"But what is the use of giving advice to a fool; no good comes of it, for:

'Advice given to fools,
Instead of calming them,
Only makes them more excited.'

—"That is what the bird found out when he gave advice to the monkey."

—"How was that?" asked Damanaka.

And Karataka told:

THE STORY OF THE MONKEY AND
A BIRD CALLED SUCHIMUKHA

"A troupe of monkeys was living somewhere in the mountains. It was winter. The rain, accompanied by a strong wind, drenched their bodies, and they shivered with cold.

"Some of the monkeys found some red Gunja* fruits and began to blow them, hoping to make fire from them.

"A bird, by the name of Suchimukha*, saw their vain attempts and said to them, 'What big fools you are! Those aren't embers of fire, they're only gunja fruits. You're wasting your time! These fruits can never protect you against the cold! Find some place to shelter, in a jungle or a cave or a burrow, where the rain and the wind can't reach you.'

—'Fool yourself!' said one of the old monkeys. 'What is it to do with you! For they say:

"A wise man who wants to succeed,
Should never give advice
To a man who has been repeatedly obstructed in his work
Or to a gambler, who has just lost his money." '

"But, disregarding what the old monkey had said, the bird persisted in asking why the monkeys were making such an effort and all to no purpose and he refused to stop his chatter. One monkey, who had become frustrated by his vain efforts, caught hold of the bird by the wings and smashed him against a stone, killing him.

—"And so," continued Karataka, "that's why I said:

'Advice given to fools,
Instead of calming them,
Only makes them more excited.
Just as giving milk to snakes
Only increases their poison.'

—"And, another thing, you should not give advice to just anyone. A furious monkey destroyed a sparrow's nest for the same reason!"

—"How was that?" asked Damanaka.

And Karataka told:

THE STORY OF THE SPARROW AND THE MONKEY

"Somewhere in the jungle, there grew a Shami* tree. On its long branches, a pair of sparrows had made their home.

"One day, in winter, whilst the pair was sitting happily together, a light rain began to fall.

"After some time, a monkey, battered by the strong winds, came and stood under the tree, his teeth chattering with cold.

"When the female sparrow saw him in this state, she said to the monkey, 'With your hands and feet, you look like a human being. So why don't you make a home for yourself?'

"The monkey got angry and shouted, 'Why don't you shut your mouth, you slut!' And then he said to himself, 'What a cheek this female bird has, giving me advice! This insolent harlot thinks, she is an educated woman and won't stop yapping. She makes me want to kill her!'

"Then the monkey said, 'Why should you worry, for they say:

"You should only give advice
To someone who specifically asks for it,
Otherwise, it's like crying in the wilderness." '

"Without much ado, the monkey climbed up the tree and tore up the nest in a thousand pieces.

—"And so," continued Karataka, "you shouldn't give advice to just any one. And in the same way," he went on, "my good advice had no effect on you, but it's not your fault, for:

'Only the good and not the bad,
Derive benefit from good advice.
Just as a bright light put into a dark, upturned
   pot
Becomes useless,
So advice given to an undeserving person,
Will be fruitless and ineffectual.'

—"The trouble with you is, you think yourself too clever. Don't you know the story of Dharmabuddhi* and Papabuddhi*? Because the son was much too clever, his father was nearly suffocated to death by the smoke!"
—"How was that?" asked Damanaka.
And Karataka told:

THE STORY OF DHARMABUDDHI
AND PAPABUDDHI

"In a village, there lived two friends, whose names were Dharmabuddhi and Papabuddhi. One day, Papabuddhi thought to himself, 'I am not only poor but also not so bright, so I shall get Dharmabuddhi's help, go with him to another kingdom and make some money. Then, I shall cheat him of his share of the fortune, and live happily ever after.'

"And so, after a few days, Papabuddhi said to Dharmabuddhi, 'My friend! How are you planning to provide for your old age? Let's go to a foreign country and make money there! Besides, unless you travel abroad, what stories will you tell your grandsons? For:

"A man who has not wandered in different lands
And has not learned foreign languages,
Nor studied various cultures,
And made himself a fortune,
Is born in vain on this earth." '

"Dharmabuddhi readily agreed to accompany Papabuddhi and carry out his plan. He took leave of his parents and, on an auspicious day, set out with Papabuddhi on their travels.

"Through Dharmabuddhi's cleverness, the two of them made a lot of money and after some time, returned home, extremely pleased with themselves.

"As they were approaching their own village, Papabuddhi said to Dharmabuddhi, 'Friend! It's not a good idea to carry all this money home, because then our friends and relatives will want a share of it. So let us take home only a nominal amount and bury the rest in the jungle. When the necessity arises, we can come back and dig it out, for they say:

"A clever man does not show off his wealth to anyone,

For even the mind of a sage
May be shaken by the sight of money." '
—'Very well then,' replied Dharmabuddhi, 'we will.'

"And so after burying most of the money, they returned home with the remainder and lived happily.

"Some time after, at dead of night, Papabuddhi went to the jungle, uncovered all the money that was buried there, took it out, and closed the pit as it had been before. Then he returned home with the money.

"After a few days, Papabuddhi went to Dharmabuddhi and said, 'Friend! I have a large family and as a result my money is all gone. Let's go and fetch some more from the place where we buried it.'
—'All right then,' replied Dharmabuddhi, 'we will.'

"When the two arrived at the place, they dug up the pit and found the money pot empty. Papabuddhi began to beat his head, crying out, 'Oh Dharmabuddhi! Only you and nobody else could have stolen the money and filled in the pit! Give me back my half or I shall make a complaint against you in the court of law.'
—'You scoundrel!' said Dharmabuddhi. 'Don't you talk like that! I am indeed Dharmabuddhi*! I could never commit such a theft! For they say:

"A righteous man looks upon other men's women
As his own mother,
And other men's wealth
As crow droppings
And other human beings
As his own self." '

"And so, fighting like this, they went to the judges and accused each other. The judges ordered them to submit themselves to trial by fire* to find out the truth.

"But Papabuddhi said to them, 'This decision is not good, for they say:

"In the investigation of disputes,
Only in the absence of written evidence and
witnesses,
Do the wise recommend ordeal by fire."

—'Now, the goddesses in the trees of the jungle near by will be my witnesses. They will be able to reveal to us, which one is a thief and which one is an honest man.'

—'You are right,' said the judges. 'We are very anxious to know the truth about this. So, tomorrow morning you must both accompany us to the jungle.'

"After that, Papabuddhi went home and said to his father, 'I have stolen a huge amount of money belonging to Dharmabuddhi and we have taken the matter to the court. Now only your co-operation will save me. Otherwise I shall lose not only the money but also my life.'

—'My son!' said the father. 'Tell me quickly what I can do to save you and make the money secure.'

—'Well,' said Papabuddhi, 'in the jungle, there is a Shami tree, which is hollow inside. You get into the hollow now so that, tomorrow morning, when we come with the judges, to find out the truth, you can shout from inside the tree, "Dharmabuddhi is the thief." '

"His father agreed to this arrangement and left immediately.

"Next morning, Papabuddhi took an early bath and accompanied by Dharmabuddhi and the judges, went to the Shami tree and asked in a loud voice, 'Oh goddess in the tree! Tell us which one is the thief.'

"Immediately Papabuddhi's father, hidden inside the hollow of the tree, replied, 'Listen! It's Dharmabuddhi who stole the money.'

"When the judges heard this, they were wonderstruck. They opened their eyes wide and immediately started discussing how to punish Dharmabuddhi according to the law.

"But, meanwhile, Dharmabuddhi put a heap of dried leaves and grass in front of the hollow of the tree and set fire to it. When the fire was blazing, out came Papabuddhi's father, crying pitifully, with half his body burnt and his eyes popping out.

—'Friend,' they all said to him, 'whatever has happened to you ?'

—'It's all Papabuddhi's fault!' he replied and he told them all that Papabuddhi had done.

"Then they hanged Papabuddhi on the same Shami tree.

"The judges praised Dharmabuddhi and said, 'It's very true what they say:

"A wise man thinks not only of a solution to his problems,
But also of its consequences.
The heron found a way to kill the snake,
Little realising that this would result in his own destruction.

—'How was that?' asked Dharmabuddhi.

And the judges told:

THE STORY OF THE FOOLISH HERON,
THE BLACK SNAKE AND THE MUNGOOSE

" 'In a jungle, there was a banyan tree. A number of herons had built their nests in it.

" 'Now, in the hollow of the tree lived a black snake. He used to eat up the heron's young, before their wings had sprouted.

" 'One heron, whose children had been eaten by the snake, came to the bank of the river Saraswati* with tears in his eyes.

" 'A crab saw him and asked, "Uncle! Why are you crying ?"

—"What can I do ?" said the heron. "I am so unlucky that all my children have been eaten up by the black snake, who lives in the hollow of the tree. I'm crying because I am heart-broken. Tell me, how could I kill the black snake ?"

" 'Now, when the crab heard this, he thought to himself, "This heron is a natural enemy of our species. What I'll do is tell him truth and lies in such a way that all the other herons will be completely destroyed. As they say:

'Let your speech be soft as butter
But your heart as hard as stone,
Advise your enemy in such a way
That he is wiped out, along with his race.' "

" 'And so, the crab said to the heron, "Uncle! If this is the case, then scatter some bits of fish and mutton from the burrow of the mungoose to the snake's hole, so that the mungoose will follow the food, reach the snake's hole and kill him."

" 'The heron listened to the crab's advice and did as he had told him to. As the crab had anticipated, the mungoose followed the trail of fish and mutton, reached the snake's hole and killed him. But unfortunately, in due course, the mungoose also killed off all the herons living on the top of the tree as well.

—'And so,' continued the judges, 'that's why we said:
     "A wise man thinks not only of a solution to his
        problems,
     But also of its consequences."

—'Papabuddhi thought of a solution but he did not
consider how it would work out. That's why he came
to grief.'

—"And so," continued Karataka, "that's why I said that
you, Damanaka, are like Papabuddhi. You too thought
of a plan—to make these two quarrel—but you did not
think of the harm that would come out of it. The fact
that you have put your master's life in danger,
demonstrates your treachery. You had better keep away
from me, for, if you can bring Pingalaka to this state,
God only knows what you will do to me. For, in a
situation like this, anything can happen. As Jveernadhana* said to the judges:
     'Where rats can eat away a heavy iron balance,
     Undoubtedly, a flamingo can also fly off with a
        child.' "

—"How was that ?" asked Damanaka.

And Karataka told:

THE STORY OF THE IRON BALANCE AND THE MERCHANT'S SON

"In a certain town, there lived a merchant's son by the name of Jveernadhana. Because he had lost all his money, he made up his mind to leave that part of the country and go somewhere else, for:

'A man who has formerly lived in great style
But now lives in great misery,
Is looked down upon by all.'

"Now in his house, the merchant's son had a very heavy iron balance, that he had inherited from his forefathers. He deposited this with another merchant and then left for a different part of the country.

"When he had travelled all over the country to his heart's content, Jveernadhana returned to his own town, went to the merchant's house and said, 'Ho! Merchant! Please return the balance that I deposited with you.'

—'But brother,' said the merchant, 'I no longer have it. The rats ate it!'

—'Merchant,' said Jveernadhana, 'if that's the case, then it is not your fault. Life is like that, nothing lasts for ever. Anyway, I am going to the river for a bath. Please let your son Dhanadeva* come with me to carry the things and look after them.'

"Now the merchant was afraid that the bath things* might be stolen, so he said to his son, 'My son! Here is your uncle. He is going to the river for a bath. Go along with him and carry the things that he needs.' It's true what they say:

"One man is kind to another,
Not only out of affection
But out of fear, greed and other reasons.
If, for no reason at all,
One man is over-attentive to another,
It's very doubtful that the situation will end well."

"And so, the merchant's son gladly accompanied

Jveernadhana to the river and carried his bath things.
When he had taken his bath, Jveernadhana caught hold
of the merchant's son and threw him into a cave near
the river bank. He then closed the entrance with a big
rock and returned quickly to the merchant's house.

"When the merchant saw him coming back alone, he
cried, 'Where is my son who went with you to the river?'
—'I am very sorry,' said Jveernadhana, 'but as he was
standing on the bank of the river, a flamingo swept
down, picked him up and flew off with him.'
—'You liar!' said the merchant. 'How could a flamingo
fly off with a child! Return my son to me immediately
or I shall complain against you in the royal court.'
—'Speaker of truth yourself,' retorted Jveernadhana,
'just as a flamingo cannot fly off with a child, so too
rats can't eat away a heavy iron balance. Give me back
my balance and I'll return your son.'

"Quarrelling like this, they went to the royal court.
The merchant began to shout, 'It's disgraceful. This
thief has kidnapped my son!'
—'Return the merchant's son to him,' the judges said
to Jveernadhana.
—'What can I do ?' he replied. 'While the child was
standing on the river bank, a flamingo swept down,
picked him up and flew off with him.'
—'You are not telling the truth!' said the judges. 'How
could a flamingo ever fly off with a child?'
—'Please listen!' said Jveernadhana. 'Where rats can eat
away a heavy iron balance, undoubtedly a flamingo can
fly off with a child!'
—'What do you mean ?' asked the judges.

And then Jveernadhana told them the whole story
from beginning to end, and the judges burst out
laughing.

"In due course they were reconciled, Jveernadhana
and the merchant. Jveernadhana got back his balance
and the merchant his son. The judges were content.
—"And so," continued Karataka, "that's why I said:

'Where rats can eat away a heavy iron balance,
Undoubtedly, a flamingo can also fly off with a
    child.'
—"Now, you Damanaka are a fool. You could not bear
to see Sanjivaka favoured by the king. That's why you
arranged this quarrel. As they say:
'Fools sneer at the wise;
The poor hate the rich,
The wicked run down the righteous,
And harlots discredit the names of virtuous women.'
—"In your foolishness, whilst trying to do good for us,
you have, in fact, done harm. That's why they say:
'A shrewd enemy is far preferable
To a foolish benefactor;
A foolish monkey killed the king
But a shrewd thief saved the lives of the
    Brahmins.' "
—"How was that ?" asked Damanaka.
And Karataka told:

THE STORY OF THE KING AND
THE FOOLISH MONKEY

"A certain king had a pet monkey. He was allowed to enter the king's palace, even when other confidential servants were forbidden to.

"One day the king was fast asleep and the monkey was fanning him. Suddenly, a fly came and sat on the king's chest. The monkey drove her away with the fan, but the fly kept coming back to the same place. The foolish monkey got excited, picked up a sword and hit at the fly with it. The fly flew away but the king was severely wounded in the chest and died as a result.

—"And so," continued Karataka, "the king who wants to live a long life, should not engage stupid servants." And now,

THE STORY OF THE THIEF AND THE BRAHMINS

"In a certain town, there lived a very learned Brahmin who, as a result of his actions in his previous life, had become a thief.

"One day, four other Brahmins, from a distant part of the country, came to that same town and started selling their wares.

"When the Brahmin-thief saw them selling these things, he said to himself, 'How can I rob these people?'

"When he had thought about it, he approached them and started quoting very eloquently from the shastras. As they say:

'A harlot pretends to be shy,
Salty water is always colder,
A hypocrite always asserts his straightforwardness,
And a crook is a charming talker.'

"In this way, the Brahmin-thief won their confidence and became their servant.

"Whilst he was in service with them, the Brahmins sold all their possessions and purchased costly jewels. In his very presence, they cut open their thighs, put all the jewels inside and then rubbed in ointment to heal the wounds. Afterwards, they began to make preparations to return to their own place.

"When the Brahmin-thief saw this, he got very worried and thought to himself, 'Oh dear, I haven't been able to rob them yet, so what I'll do is travel with them, poison them on the way and collect all the jewels.'

"With this in his mind, he went to the Brahmins, weeping pitifully.

—'Friends,' he implored them, 'you will soon be going away and leaving me here all alone. My heart has become so attached to yours with bonds of love, that the mere thought of separation from you, throws me into despair. Please take pity on me and let me come with you.'

"The Brahmins felt moved by his entreaties and took

him with them.

"On the way, the five of them came to a town called Palipura*, belonging to the Kirata* tribe. As soon as they entered the town, the crows began to scream out to the inhabitants, 'Oh! Quick, quick! The rich are coming! Kill them and take their treasure!'

"When the Kirata hunters heard the crows screaming, they rushed upon the five Brahmins, beat them up with cudgels, searching them, and removing their clothes. But they found nothing. Then they said, 'Travellers! Never have the crows proved to be wrong! You have got the treasure somewhere! Give it to us or we'll kill you, take off your skins and search every part of your body, until we find the treasure!'

"When the Brahmin-thief heard this, he thought to himself, 'If the Kirata hunters kill the Brahmins, search their bodies and take out the jewels, they will naturally kill me too. I am going to die either way, so what I'll do is, offer them my body first, let them kill me and see that there are no jewels hidden in my body and so save the lives of these four Brahmins, and their jewels too. As they say:

"My child! Why are you afraid of Yama?
He won't spare you because you are frightened!
Perhaps today, perhaps after a thousand years,
Death will certainly catch up with you." '

"And so, having made this firm resolution, the Brahmin-thief said to the Kirata hunters, 'All right then, kill me first and search me!'

"Accordingly, the Kirata hunters killed him and searched his body, but they found nothing and the four Brahmins were allowed to continue their journey.

—"And so," continued Karataka, "that's why I said:

'A shrewd enemy is far preferable
To a foolish benefactor;
A foolish monkey killed the king
But a shrewd thief saved the lives of the Brahmins.' "

Whilst Damanaka and Karataka were talking, Pingalaka and Sanjivaka started fighting. Sanjivaka's body was torn to pieces by Pingalaka's strong claws and he fell to the ground, dead.

When Pingalaka saw him dead, he thought of his good qualities and he was heart-broken. He repented killing the bullock and said to himself, "I have committed a great sin in killing Sanjivaka. For there is no greater sin than treachery. As they say:

'He who betrays a trusting friend,
Shall remain in Naraka*
For as long as the sun and moon
Continue to shine.' "

Whilst Pingalaka was thus bewailing Sanjivaka's death, Damanaka approached him in jubilant mood, and said, "Master, you have killed a treacherous grass-eater, and now you are crying! Such behaviour is not proper for a king—only weaklings behave like that. They say:

'The wise
Do not dwell on the dead
Or the living.' "

In this way, Pingalaka was pacified by Damanaka. He appointed Damanaka as minister and ruled over his kingdom.

THE END
OF THE FIRST TANTRA

WINNING OF FRIENDS

Now, this is the beginning of the second tantra, called "Winning of friends." And here is the first verse:

"Clever people and those well versed in nitishastras,
Even when they are without means,
Achieve success very quickly
Just like the crow, the mouse, the turtle and the stag."

This is how the story goes:

In the south of India, there was a city called Mahilaropyam. Not far from the city, there stood a very big tree. All kinds of birds ate its fruits and many travellers rested under its shade.

Now, on the branches of the tree, there lived a crow, by the name of Laghupatanaka*. One day, as he was flying towards the city in search of food, his eyes fell upon a black hunter, creeping towards that very tree. He looked like a servant of Yama.

When Laghupatanaka saw this, he was scared, thinking to himself, "Heavens! This wicked hunter is going to our tree! The birds who are living there will certainly come to some harm."

And so, the crow flew back to the tree and said, "Ho friends! There's a wicked hunter coming and he has brought a net and rice grains with him. Don't touch the rice! Treat it like poison."

Meanwhile, the hunter had reached the tree. He spread out his net, scattered the shining white rice on the ground underneath and hid himself near by. As the birds had been warned in advance by Laghupatanaka, they did not touch the rice and avoided being caught in the hunter's net.

Now, Chitragreeva*, the king of the doves, happened to be flying in the neighbourhood at that time. He and his retinue were looking for food. They came to this

tree and saw the ripe grains of rice. Laghupatanaka
warned them in the same way, not to touch it, but they
took no notice of him, and Chitragreeva and his entire
court were caught in the net. As they say:
  "This is what happens
  When fate is hostile
  And it's nobody's fault:
  When disaster is imminent,
  A man's mind is in turmoil,
  Even his wits fail him."
When the hunter saw that he had caught the doves,
he was overjoyed and went up to the tree. Seeing him
coming, Chitragreeva said to his retinue, "Don't be
afraid, for they say:
  'He who holds on to his courage,
  In the face of disaster,
  Will, with the help of his intelligence,
  Ultimately surmount all his difficulties.'
—"And so, let us all unite, lift the net together and fly
off with it, for they say:
  'Small things united become strong:
  Even delicate threads of cotton,
  Woven together,
  Are very hard to break.'
—"Then, when we are out of the hunter's sight, we can
free ourselves. But unless we do this quickly, we shall
all be dead!"
The doves followed Chitragreeva's plan. When the
hunter saw them flying away with his net, he ran after
them, saying to himself, "These doves have united and
are flying away with my net, but should they quarrel
on the way, they will all fall to the ground."
Laghupatanaka, the crow, was so curious to know what
would happen that he forgot all about his food and
followed the doves.
When the hunter saw the doves vanishing out of sight,
he sadly recited the following shloka*:
  "Nothing happens that is not predestined,

And what is predestined, always comes to pass,
Even when a man has something in his hand,
If fate is hostile, it slips from his grasp."
—"That's why I have lost not only the doves but my
net too, the means of supporting my family."

When Chitragreeva saw the hunter disappearing out
of sight, he said to the doves, "Friends, the wicked
hunter is not following us any more, so we can all fly
to Mahilaropyam with our minds easy. Now, I have a
friend living there, a mouse, by the name of Hiranyaka*.
He will certainly bite through these meshes and set us
free. As they say:

'When calamity befalls a man,
Only a true friend will help him;
Others offer only lip-sympathy.' "

The doves agreed to Chitragreeva's suggestion and
made their way to the mouse's home.

Now the hole, where Hiranyaka was living, had
innumerable entries and exits. For the mouse, it was an
excellent stronghold—he lived there quite fearlessly. As
they say:

"A snake without tangs,
An elephant without fury
And a king without a castle,
Are helpless,
But a single archer, behind a castle wall,
Can withstand a hundred men of the enemy."

When Chitragreeva reached the hole, he called loudly,
"Ho! Friend Hiranyaka! Come out quickly! I am in a
bad spot."

But the mouse did not come out, instead he asked
from inside, "Who are you? What do you want from
me? Tell me, what is your problem?"

—"My dear friend!" replied the king of doves. "It's
Chitragreeva, the king of the doves! Please come out
quickly, it's very urgent."

When Hiranyaka recognised his friend's voice, he came
out immediately, beaming with delight, but when he saw

the king of doves and his retinue, all caught in the net,
his face fell and he asked, "What is the meaning of
this?"

—"Hiranyaka, why ask me?" replied the king of doves.
"You know me well enough to know that it's my love
of food that has got me into this state."

—"No, my dear friend," said the mouse, "it's the will
of fate. As they say:

'When destiny so decides,
However high the birds soar in the sky,
They see the mutton, but not the trap,
And however deep the fish swim in the water,
They are caught in the fisherman's net.
Yama stretches his hand in every direction
And seizes both the wicked and the just,
He makes no distinction.' "

When he had finished speaking, Hiranyaka began to
free the king of the doves. But Chitragreeva stopped
him and said, "Don't do that! Free my followers first
and me afterwards."

—"Good heavens, no!" said Hiranyaka impatiently. "The
master comes first and then the servants!"

—"My dear friend," replied Chitragreeva, "don't talk
like that! All these trapped doves left their homes and
families to follow me. The least I can do is show them
this much consideration. They say:

'When a king shows respect to his servants,
They will never forsake him
In times of distress.'

—"Besides, your teeth might break while you're biting
my meshes through or the hunter may arrive. In both
cases, I shall be the only one free and my followers will
still be prisoners. And they say:

'When a master enjoys life
While his devoted servants suffer,
He will surely have to pay,
Both here and in hell.' "

When Hiranyaka heard this, he was very happy and

he said, "My friend, I too know a king's duties very well. I just wanted to test you. So, I shall free your followers first and, for this noble action, they will always continue to respect you as their king."

Then Hiranyaka bit through all the meshes of the net and set the doves free. Then he said to Chitragreeva, "Now, should you ever get into a similar situation again, you can come to me."

Chitragreeva thanked the mouse heartily, took his leave and flew off with his court. Hiranyaka also went back into his hole. It's very true what they say:

"A wise man should develop friendship
With the right kind of people,
For, with their help, even difficult problems
Can be tackled easily."

Now, Laghupatanaka, the crow, had seen all that had taken place and he was amazed. "How talented the mouse is!" he thought. "He actually succeeded in freeing the doves! Now, if I was caught in a trap one day, Hiranyaka could free me too. So I shall make friends with him, just in case. As they say:

'However great the volume of the sea,
It must await the appearance of full moon
To produce the high tide,
And however talented a wise man may be,
He nonetheless needs friends.' "

So the crow flew down to the mouse's hole. Imitating Chitragreeva's voice, he called, "Ho, Hiranyaka! Please come out!"

When the mouse heard this voice, he thought to himself, "Is there still a dove left in the net, calling for my help?"

However, he did not come out, but called from inside, "Who is it?"

—"It's a crow called Laghupatanaka," replied the crow.

—"Then, be off with you!" cried the mouse.

—"But I have something very important to say to you!" replied the crow. "Why won't you come out and meet me?"

—"Why should I?" replied Hiranyaka.

—"But, my friend, said the crow, "I saw how you freed
Chitragreeva and I respect you for it. One day I might
be caught in a net and you could free me too. So, I
should like to make friends with you."

—"But you are a hunter and I am your prey," replied
the mouse. "How can I be your friend? Be off! How
can anyone make friends with an enemy! As they say:

'Friendship is only possible
Between people who are equals
In strength, wealth and status.' "

—"Well," replied the crow, "if you won't make friends
with me, I'll starve myself to death, right here, at your
door!"

—"But how can I be your friend?" repeated Hiranyaka.
"You are my enemy! And it's so true what they say:

'However much you heat water,
It still extinguishes fire.' "

—"But mouse," said the crow, "until today, we have
never had the opportunity to meet each other. How
then can you possibly speak of enmity between us?"

—"There are two types of enmity," said the mouse.
"The hereditary enmity that exists between certain
species and the enmity that arises as a result of some
quarrel! As they say:

'Enmity that arises for some particular reason,
Vanishes when the cause is removed,
But the natural enmity, between certain species,
Endures for ever.
So with fire and water,
Carnivorous animals and grass-eaters,
Lions and elephants,
The mongoose and the snake,
Dogs and cats,
The hunter and the deer,
Devils and angels,
Atheists and believers,

The fools and the learned,
The immoral and the virtuous,
And a man's two wives.' "
—"But this natural enmity is pointless," said the crow.
"Friendship or enmity should develop because there's
some reason for it. And in our case, there is no reason
whatsoever for us to be enemies. So make friends with
me. They say:
'Friendship with the wicked
Is like an earthenware pot:
It is easily broken in pieces
And cannot be cemented together again,
But friendship with the good
Is like a pot made of gold,
It breaks only with great difficulty
And can easily be repaired.
Friendship with the wicked
Is like the morning shadows,
Which, to begin with, are the longest,
But decrease with the passage of time,
Whilst friendship with the good
Is like the shadows at noon,
Which, at first, are very small,
But increase as time goes on.'
—"Now, I swear to God, Hiranyaka, that I will do you
no harm!"
—"Even so, I can't trust you," said the mouse. "For
they say:
'Never put your trust in someone
Who is not to be trusted.
Nor even in a trustworthy man
Beyond limit.
A weakling who is wary,
Escapes being killed by the strongest of men,
But a strong man, who puts too much faith in
    others,
Can be killed by a mere weakling.' "
When Laghupatanaka heard this clever reply from the

mouse, he was amazed at Hiranyaka's knowledge of
nitishastras and was at a loss for an answer. Then he
said to the mouse, "Oh, all right then, if you still don't
trust me, stay inside your hole, but please talk to me a
bit, speak about politics and moral stories."

When the mouse heard this, he thought to himself,
"This crow, Laghupatanaka, seems to be very intelligent
and perhaps he is even telling the truth. I think I will
make friends with him."

Then the mouse said, "All right then, my friend, I
agree!"

And so, from that day onward, the two of them became
good friends. The crow would bring fruits and delicacies
for the mouse and the mouse, in return, would save a
few titbits for the crow. And they would entertain each
other, telling stories. As they say:

"The indications of friendship are
    Mutual entertainment
    And the exchange of confidences and presents."
And,
    "Unless you offer oblations to the gods,
    Your wishes will not be fulfilled."

In the course of time, the mouse trusted the crow so
much that he would even sit under his wings and talk
to him.

But one day, the crow came to the mouse with tears
in his eyes and said, "Oh Hiranyaka, I feel absolutely
fed up with this part of the country! I would like to
fly off to some other place."

—"But, my dear fellow," said the mouse, "why do you
say that?"

—"Listen, Hiranyaka," said Laghupatanaka, "there has
been no rain here for a long time and, as a result, the
people don't have enough to eat. As they haven't
sufficient for themselves, they don't feed the crows any
more. On the contrary, they have set traps everywhere
to catch us. I myself was caught in one of those traps,
but I was destined to live longer and so managed to

free myself. So that is the reason, why I am fed up
with this country. And I am shedding these tears because,
if I leave and go somewhere else, I must also leave such
a good friend as you are."

—"Where do you mean to go?" asked the mouse.

—"Well," replied Laghupatanaka, "further south, deep
in the jungle, is a lake. A very dear friend of mine, a
turtle, by the name of Mantharaka*, lives there. He
feeds me on bits of fish and I can pass my time very
happily with him, discussing moral tales and talking
philosophy. I can't bear to stay here and see the
destruction of my own people. As they say:

'Blessed indeed are those
    Who do not see the destruction of their land and
        family
    Due to drought and the ruination of crops.'

—"So, I would prefer to leave and go somewhere else.'

—"I would like to come with you," said the mouse, "for,
I too have experienced something dreadful here."

—"What do you mean?" said the crow. "Explain to me."

—"It's a very long story," said the mouse. "I'll tell you
about it, when we arrive at your friend's place."

—"But," said the crow, "I shall be flying in the air and
you will be crawling on the land, so how can you
accompany me?"

—"Well," replied the mouse, "you can carry me on your
back and take me. For me there is no other way of
getting there."

When the crow heard this, he said delightedly, "Well,
if that's the case, I'm a very lucky fellow, for I shall be
able to enjoy your company over there too. Let's go
immediately. So, get on my back and hold on tight, and
I shall take you there without any difficulty."

And so, the mouse seated himself firmly on the crow's
back and the crow started the journey to the lake. Flying
slowly, by stages, the crow and the mouse finally arrived
at the lake.

The turtle saw the crow and the mouse come flying

down and he was so astonished that he plunged headlong into the water.

The crow saw what had happened and landed at the bottom of a tree. The mouse jumped down to the ground and crept into a hole. Then the crow seated himself on a branch of the tree and shouted, "Ho, Mantharaka! It's your friend, Laghupatanaka, the crow! Come out quickly and give me a big hug!"

When the turtle heard his voice, he recognised Laghupatanaka and came out of the water. He was overcome with emotion and cried, "Laghupatanaka! Welcome! Please forgive me for not recognising you straightaway, but it's so long since I saw you."

Then the crow flew down to meet the turtle. They hugged each other delightedly and spent some time telling each other about their experiences. The mouse too came out of the hole, bowed before Mantharaka and sat down.

When the turtle saw the mouse, he turned to Laghupatanaka and said, "My friend! Who is this mouse? You feed on mice, so why have you brought this one along with you, on your back! You must have some definite reason for it."

—"Mantharaka," replied the crow, "this mouse is a very dear friend of mine. His name is Hiranyaka. He is even dearer to me than my own life. He is always gay but, at the moment, he is very sad and dejected."

—"Why?" asked Mantharaka.

—"I've already asked him about it," said the crow, "but he said that it was a long story and so he would prefer to tell it here beside the lake."

The crow then turned to the mouse and said, "Now, my dear friend Hiranyaka, what about your story?"

And, by way of reply, Hiranyaka told:

THE STORY OF THE SADHU AND THE MOUSE

"In the southern part of the country, there is a city called Mahilaropyam. Not far from the city, there was a temple dedicated to Shiva. A Sadhu*, by the name of Tamrachuda*, used to live in this temple. Everyday he would go into the city for alms and in this way, he supported himself.

"When the Sadhu had finished his evening meals, he would put what was left over in a begging bowl and hang it up. Then he would go to sleep. In the morning he gave this food to the workers, who in return cleaned and swept the living place.

"Now one day, my friends, the other mice said to me, 'Hiranyaka! The Sadhu is afraid that we will take his cooked food, so he puts it in a begging bowl and hangs it up on a peg, so that we cannot reach it. But you are so good at jumping that you can reach the bowl very easily. Why should we have to go to the bother of searching for food elsewhere when, with your help, we can enjoy what is here.'

"And so, I agreed to the plan and we crept to the place together and found the begging bowl hanging there. I reached it without any difficulty and threw some food down to my friends, standing below. Then I had my share. Afterwards we all crept back to our homes. In this way, we enjoyed the food night after night.

"When the Sadhu noticed that his food was being stolen, he hung his begging bowl still higher. However, the minute he went to sleep, somehow or other, I reached the begging bowl and we did as usual.

"Finally he thought of a plan to put a stop to my mischief. When he was wide awake, he would beat the begging bowl with a split bamboo stick to frighten me off. The minute he went to sleep, I would try to reach the food as usual but somehow or other he would wake up and hit the begging bowl again. I would run away as fast as I could but come back again after some time. In this way, we would spend the entire night, fighting.

"One day, a Sanyasi, by the name of Brihatsphinga*, who was on a pilgrimage, came to the temple to see his friend Tamrachuda. The Sadhu welcomed him with open arms and was very hospitable towards him. Before they finally went to bed, they talked about religion. But as the Sadhu was thinking of us, mice, he kept hitting out at the begging bowl with the split bamboo stick. He was not attentive to the Sanyasi and so he gave only abstract and absent-minded replies. Suddenly the Sanyasi said angrily, 'Tamrachuda! It is now clear to me that you are no true friend of mine. You are giving me vague and abstract replies. Now that you have a temple of your own, you have become proud. You have forgotten our old friendship and the love you had for me. For such behaviour you deserve to go to hell. They say, "A householder should welcome a guest with the following words, 'Please take a seat and make yourself comfortable. You have visited me after many days. Tell me, what's the latest news? Your are looking rather thin. Are you well?' But,

"A man who visits a house
Where his host, seeing him enter,
Continues to look absent-mindedly,
Here and there and on the ground
And answers with only half his attention,
Such a guest is an ox without horns*."

—'Indeed, I can't put up with such behaviour! I shall leave this very minute and go somewhere else.'

"Tamrachuda was shocked to hear the Sanyasi talking like this and he said to him humbly, 'Bhagawan, please don't talk like that. You are my dearest friend. Please listen and I shall tell you the reason for my inattention. Every day, whatever is left over from my food, I put in a begging bowl and hang it high on a peg. But there's a mouse that, somehow or other, manages to

reach it. He eats something from it himself, then throws
the rest down to the other mice. As a result, in the
morning there is no food for the workers and they
refuse to clean the place. That's why I have been hitting
this begging bowl, to frighten the mice off. This is the
only reason for my lack of attention to you. For jumping,
this wicked mouse even puts a cat and a monkey to
shame.'

—'Do you know where the mouse lives?' asked the
Sanyasi.

—'No, I do not,' said the Sadhu.

—'Well,' went on the Sanyasi, 'this mouse, wherever he
may be living, must certainly have accumulated quite a
lot of food, and this gives him a feeling of exaltation
and consequently the energy to jump so high. They say:

    "When a man is wealthy,
      He becomes elated
      And his energy increases."

—'For every action there is an explanation. As they say:

    "Mother Shandili* had a reason
      When she tried to change
      The husked sesame seeds
      For unhusked ones." '

—'How was that?' asked the Sadhu.

And the Sanyasi told:

THE STORY OF MOTHER SHANDILI

" 'Once, during the monsoon season, I requested a Brahmin to allow me to stay with him, so that I could fast and pray undisturbed. He agreed, and I went to his home.

" 'One day, I was listening attentively to the conversation the Brahmin was having with his wife. "Brahmini*," he said to her, "tomorrow is a special festival, it's Sankranti*, a very favourable time for collecting alms. So I shall go to one of the villages to beg. And you too should give something to a Brahmin."

" 'The Brahmini got excited when she heard him say this. "How can we afford to give something to a Brahmin when we are so poor ourselves!" she exclaimed. "And another thing, ever since I married you, I have had no luck whatsoever. I have never had any good food to eat or any good clothes to wear and you've never bought me a single ornament!"

" 'When the Brahmin heard this, his spirits were very dampened and he said, "Oh, Brahmini, when you have only a mouthful, you should give half of it to someone in need. They say:

'An insignificant person who gives,
Is respected by all,
But not so a rich man who is miserly.
Sweet water from a small well quenches the thirst,
But not the salty water of the great ocean.' "

—"Well," said the Brahmin's wife, "I have got a few sesame seeds. I'll take the husks off them and make them into a tasty dish for some Brahmin."

" 'And so, early next morning, when the Brahmin had left for the next village, his wife cleaned the sesame seeds in hot water, removed the husks and put them in the sun to dry. Then she got busy with her household work.

" 'Meanwhile, a dog came along and cocked his leg

up over the sesame seeds and went away. When the Brahmini saw what had happened, she said, "Fate has turned against me! What a trick to play! Well, I'll take the seeds to some other house and exchange them for some unhusked seeds, anyone will agree to such an exchange."

—'And so,' continued the Sanyasi, 'mother Shandili went off to exchange them. Now, she happened to go to the very house that I was visiting that morning to collect alms. She said to the lady of the house, "Would you like to change these husked sesame seeds for unhusked ones?"

" 'The lady of the house was just about to make the exchange when her son stopped her, quoting from the Kamandaki* nitishastra. "Mother!" he went on. "There must be some reason for mother Shandili to be trying to exchange these husked sesame seeds. Don't agree to it!"

" 'When mother Shandili saw that she had failed, she quietly left the house and returned home.

—'And so,' continued the Sanyasi, 'that's why I said, that for every action there is always an explanation. And the explanation for this mouse's supernatural jumping power lies in his vast accumulation of food. Now, you say you don't know where he comes from.'

—'No, Bhagawan!' said the Sadhu.

—'Do you have a pickaxe?' asked the Sanyasi.

—'Yes,' said the Sadhu. 'I have an iron one.'

—'Well,' said the Sanyasi, 'early tomorrow morning, both of us will follow the mouse's tracks, find his hole and dig up his store of food.'

"Now when I heard this, I thought to myself, 'I am done for. What this Sanyasi says is logical and I am quite sure that they will find my hoarding place, for they say:

"A wise man can weigh another's strength
By a mere glance
And estimate the weight of an object

Simply by handling it." '

"So trembling with fear and accompanied by my
followers, I avoided the usual way home and led them
by a devious route, to try to mislead the Sadhu and the
Sanyasi.

"All of a sudden, there, right in front of us, was a
big tomcat. He pounced headlong, killed some of us
and injured others. Those who managed to survive,
returned to their holes, cursing me all the way for
having led them into this. The floor was covered with
the blood of the injured and the dead. It's true what
they say:

'When Fate is hostile,
What can you achieve
By making an effort to avoid it?'

"I was very upset by this incident and afterwards, I
went off somewhere on my own.

"After some time, the wicked Sanyasi, accompanied by
the Sadhu, followed the track of blood, searching for
mouse holes. He chanced to arrive at the entrance of
my hole and began to dig the ground. While he was
digging, he found the hoard of food that I had been
guarding all these days, whose possession made me
exalted and gave me the energy to jump and reach
such difficult places. Then, taking the hoard of food
with them, the two returned to the temple.

"When I reached my hole, I could not bear to look
at the desolate place. I began to think, 'What shall I
do? Where shall I go? How can I find peace of mind?'
Absorbed in such thoughts, I spent a miserable night.

"As the sun set, I made my way to the temple, deeply
dejected. My followers came with me. When Tamrachuda
heard the noise we made, he began to hit the begging
bowl with the split bamboo stick.

—'My dear fellow,' said his guest, 'why don't you relax
and go to bed?'

—'Bhagawan,' replied the Sadhu, 'that wicked mouse
and his gang are back again! That's why I am hitting

the bowl.'

—'My friend,' said his guest with a smile, 'don't worry. After losing his hoard of food, this mouse will also have lost his energy to jump. All creatures react in the same way, for:

"To flaunt oneself, to humble others,
And to treat them contemptuously,
All this is done on the strength of riches." '

"When I heard this, I felt very annoyed and jumped at the begging bowl, but I missed it and fell to the ground.

"When my enemy heard me fall, he laughed heartily and said to Tamrachuda, 'Look, Look! How funny! See how he is staggering about! Without his riches, this mouse has become as ordinary as any of the others in his gang. Now, go to sleep and let your mind be at rest. We have, in our hands, the source of his energy to jump. They say:

"A snake without fangs
And a man without money,
Merely exist." '

"When I heard this, I said to myself, 'Yes, my enemy is quite right. I can hardly jump. Cursed is the life of a fellow who is deprived of his riches. As they say:

"A rich man
Who loses his money,
Suffers more than a poor man
Who never had any." '

"Now, while I was there, I discovered that my enemy was keeping my hoard of food in a small bag and using it for a pillow. I was very upset.

"By the time I returned home, it was morning. When my followers saw me, they began to whisper to each other, 'He's incapable of leading us properly. By following him, we shall only fall a prey to fat cats. What is the good of having a leader like that, for:

"A master from whom one derives no benefits,
Should be avoided from a long distance." '

"When I heard them say this, I went quietly into my hole. Nobody came near me and I thought to myself, 'Curse poverty, for:

"The life of a man without riches,
A marriage without children,
Oblations to dead parents without a Brahmin's
    rituals
And religious ceremonies without gifts to charity,
All these are futile." '

"While I was thinking this, my followers chose another leader. Seeing me utterly deserted, they began to make fun of me.

"By now, it was evening. Half asleep, I began to think, 'I shall try to enter the temple tonight while the Sadhu is fast asleep and slowly drag away the pillow and my hoard of food. In this way, I shall regain my former status. And even if I lose my life in the attempt, it will be worth it.'

"So I went back to the temple. I reached the bag and stealthily began to pull at it, but somehow the Sadhu woke up and hit out at me with the split bamboo stick. I was destined to live longer, so I escaped the blow. It's said:

'You always get
What's coming to you.
Even the gods can't oppose
The laws of destiny.
And so, I regret nothing
And nothing astonishes me.
What destiny gives me,
No one can take away.'

—"How was that? asked the crow and the turtle. And the mouse told:

THE STORY OF THE MERCHANT'S SON

"In a certain town, there lived a merchant whose name was Sagaradatta*. He had one son. One day, the young man bought a book that was being sold for a hundred rupees*. Inside the book, the only thing written was a single verse. It went like this:

'You always get
What's coming to you.
Even the gods can't oppose
The laws of destiny.
And so, I regret nothing
And nothing astonishes me.
What destiny gives me,
No one can take away.'

"When Sagaradatta saw his son's book, he asked him, 'How much did you pay for this book?'

—'A hundred rupees,' replied his son.

—'You stupid fellow!' said his father. 'You ought to be ashamed of yourself. If you pay a hundred rupees for a book with only one verse in it, how will you fare in business! From today onward never enter my house again!'

"With these harsh words, he drove him out of the house.

"Utterly dejected, the merchant's son went off to another city to settle down there.

"After a few days, one of the residents said to him, 'What's your name and where do you come from?'

—'You always get what's coming to you,' he replied.

"And whoever asked him the same question received the same reply. And so, the merchant's son came to be known by the name of 'Get-what's-coming-to-you.'

"One day, a young and very beautiful princess, whose name was Chandravati*, accompanied by a lady-in-waiting, went to a certain festival in the city. While she was there, by chance her eyes fell on a very handsome prince and immediately Kamadeva* fired an arrow into her heart.

"The princess turned to her lady-in-waiting and said, 'Find a way for me to meet this prince!'

"And so, the lady-in-waiting went up to the prince and said, 'The princess Chandravati has sent me to speak to you. This is the message she sends, "The minute I saw you, Kamadeva's arrow pierced my heart. Come to me quickly or I shall die." '

—'But how can I enter the palace to meet the princess?' said the prince.

—'Well,' replied the lady-in-waiting, 'when it's dark, you will find a rope hanging from one of the windows of the palace. You can climb up on it and get into the princess's room.'

—'Well,' replied the prince, 'if the princess really wants me to, I shall certainly come.'

"However when the time came, the prince thought to himself, 'It would be very wicked of me to meet the princess like this, for they say:

'A wise man should avoid doing anything
Which may bring dishonour, humiliation
Or exclusion from heaven." '

"And so, having thought the matter over carefully, the prince decided not to go to the princess.

"Meanwhile, Get-what's-coming-to-you was wandering about in the dark, when he came across the white palace and saw the rope hanging down. Curious to know what it was for, he caught hold of it and climbed up.

"When he arrived at the princess's window, as it was dark, she took it for granted that it was the prince. She received him warmly, gave him food and drink and entertained him lavishly.

"Afterwards, she said to him, 'I fell in love with you at first sight and I belong to you, body and soul. In my heart I shall never have any husband except you. But why don't you speak to me?'

—'You always get what's coming to you, replied the

merchant's son.

"Perplexed by this curious reply, the princess took a closer look at her companion and realised that it was not the prince at all. She was furious and turned him out immediately, making him descend the same way he had gone up. Get-what's-coming-to-you meekly made his way to an old temple near by and went to sleep.

"Now, a night watchman, who had made an appointment with a woman of bad character in the same dilapidated temple, woke him up and asked him, 'Who are you?'

—'You always get what's coming to you,' replied the merchant's son.

"Now, this watchman wanted to cover up his own wicked carryings-on, so he said to Get-what's-coming-to-you, 'This is a very broken-down old temple, no one ever stays here. You had better go over to my house and rest there.' And he pointed out his house. Get-what's-coming-to-you agreed and went there.

"However, he entered the wrong room. In this room, the watchman's beautiful daughter, whose name was Vinayavati*, was waiting for her lover, with whom she had made an appointment. When Get-what's-coming-to-you appeared on the scene, it was pitch dark. Thinking it was her lover, the girl married him according to Gandharva rites*. Afterwards she asked him, 'Why don't you talk to me?'

—'You always get what's coming to you,' he replied.

"As soon as Vinayavati heard this, she realised that it was not her lover at all but someone else, and she thought to herself, 'Whenever you rush into something, without thinking about it sufficiently, this sort of thing happens.' Then she cursed Get-what's-coming-to-you and threw him out of the house.

"When he came out, he saw a huge marriage procession passing by. The bridegroom, whose name was Vara-keerti*, was coming from another village to get married.

"Get-what's-coming-to-you   joined   the   procession

making its way to the bride's house.

"Now the bride's father had got a special rostrum erected on the main highway for the marriage ceremony and the bride was seated on it in magnificent clothes and jewels, waiting for the bridegroom.

"Suddenly, a mad elephant, who had already killed his master, appeared on the scene. When they saw him, one and all ran helter-skelter to safety. But the bride was too terrified to move.

"When Get-what's-coming-to-you saw this, he rushed to her and said, 'Don't be afraid, I'll protect you!' And he took hold of her left hand and pacified her. Then he pulled a huge nail out of the rostrum and very courageously went up to the elephant and jabbed the nail into him. As luck would have it, the elephant got frightened and ran away.

"After some time, the bridegroom, along with his friends and relatives, returned to the scene. When he saw someone else holding the bride's hand, he said to her father, 'Look here! You promised me this girl's hand and now you have given her away to someone else.'

—'Listen!' replied the girl's father, 'I was so terrified when the elephant appeared that I ran off, like the rest of you. I really don't know what happened during my absence.' Then he turned to his daughter and said, 'What did happen? Tell me!' She replied, 'When my life was in danger, this man showed great courage and saved me. Now, I will marry no one but him.'

"After this, the whole night elapsed in argument.

"By morning, the whole city was humming with the news. The king and the princess also heard about it and came personally.

"The night watchman's daughter also heard the news and arrived on the scene.

—'What's all this about?' the king asked Get-what's-coming-to-you. 'Explain to me.'

—'You always get what's coming to you,' he replied.

"When the princess heard this reply, she immediately remembered the previous night's incident and thought to herself.

'Even the gods can't oppose
The laws of destiny.'

"When the night watchman's daughter heard his reply, she too remembered the previous night's happenings and said,

'And so, I regret nothing
And nothing astonishes me.'

"And when the bride heard his reply, she said,

'What destiny gives me,
No one can take away.'

"When the king heard them talking like this, he felt that there was something mysterious behind it all and he insisted on knowing the truth. The princess and the two girls told him in detail exactly what had happened between them and Get-what's-coming-to-you.

"Then, with great pomp and ceremony, the king gave the princess in marriage to Get-what's-coming-to-you and presented him with a thousand villages and all sorts of ornaments. As he had no son, he appointed Get-what's-coming-to-you as his heir-apparent to the throne.

"The night watchman also gave Get-what's-coming-to-you his daughter in marriage, with a dowry such as he could afford.

"The merchant also gave Get-what's-coming-to-you his daughter in marriage and showered him with presents.

"When it was all over, Get-what's-coming-to-you arranged for his parents and relatives to be brought to him and they all lived happily ever after.

—"And so," continued the mouse, "that's why I said:

'You always get
What's coming to you.
Even the gods can't oppose
The laws of destiny.
And so, I regret nothing
And nothing astonishes me.

> What destiny gives me,
> No one can take away.'

—"Now I had suffered deeply at the temple and I was
very unhappy. I did not feel that it was worth staying
in that place, that's why I came here with
Laghupatanaka."

—"My friend," said Mantharaka, the turtle, "this crow
has been a real friend to you. He is your natural enemy
and yet even though he was hungry because of the
famine, he brought you here safely on his back. He
could well have eaten you on the way, but he didn't.
He is your true friend. As they say:

> 'When you are rich,
> All men are your friends,
> But when calamity strikes,
> Only a true friend stands by you.'

—"So live here on the bank of this river and consider
it your home. Don't worry because you are no longer
rich, for they say:

> 'You can only enjoy riches and youth,
> The friendship of the wicked,
> Cooked food and women,
> For a short time.'

And,

> 'Money is troublesome to earn
> And more troublesome to guard.
> Getting it or spending it, brings unhappiness.
> Money is a curse!'

—"Now you, Hiranyaka," continued Mantharaka, "are
obviously a wise fellow, and they say:

> 'A wise man uses his wits
> To make money
> But avoids being a miser,
> For he may be destined to lose his money:
> The art is in learning how to enjoy it.
> This is what Somilaka* learned in the deep jungle.' "

—"How was that?" asked the mouse and the crow.
And Mantharaka told:

THE STORY OF SOMILAKA

"In a certain town, there lived a weaver by the name of Somilaka. The cloth he wove was so exquisite that it was fit to be worn by kings. But somehow, he could earn only just enough to make two ends meet. On the other hand, the other weavers, who produced inferioɪ cloth, had become very rich.

"Seeing this, the weaver said to his wife, 'My dear, look at this! These weavers produce inferior cloth and yet they have become rich, while I remain poor. I am fed up with this place! I mean to go to some other kingdom and make money there.'

—'My dear husband,' replied his wife, 'you're quite wrong in thinking that you will earn money somewhere else, when you can't make it here, for they say:

"What is not predestined,
Do what you will,
Can never happen:
What is not predestined,
Will even come into your hand
And yet slip away:
But what destiny has planned,
Will surely come to pass
Without your help:
For destiny and action
Go hand in hand,
The one is as much a part of the other,
As light and shade."

And,
"As a calf will find out its mother
Amongst a thousand cows.
So destiny selects its performers
From amongst the masses."

—'And so,' continued his wife, 'carry on working here.'
—'My dear,' said the weaver, 'what you say isn't true, for they say:

"No plan can succeed,
Without determined effort,
Any more than you can clap with one hand."
—'Even if destiny makes food available, you have to
stretch out your hand and take it. It does not fall into
your mouth, any more than a deer falls into the mouth
of a reclining lion. It's the people who make a determined
effort who succeed. As they say:

"Lakshmi bestows her favours,
On the zealous man,
She scorns the idle,
Who depend entirely on luck.
So, brush destiny aside
And try with all your might.
If you still fail,
Find out what went wrong."
—'And so, my dear,' continued the weaver, 'I have made
up my mind to go somewhere else.'

"Soon afterwards, the weaver left his home town and
went to Vardhamanapura*.

"He lived there for three years and earned three
hundred pieces of gold. Then he started off on his
journey home.

"He was half way home, and still deep in the jungle,
when the sun set. For fear of the wild animals, he
climbed up a big banyan tree and went to sleep there.
While he slept, he had a dream. He saw two
terrifying-looking people, arguing with each other.
—'Action!' said one of them to the other. 'Why did you
allow Somilaka to earn three hundred pieces of gold?
Don't you know that he is destined to earn only what
he requires for his food and clothing?'
—'Destiny!' replied the other. 'What could I do? This
man put in a great effort and I had to reward him
according to his actions. But it is still for you to decide
how much he is going to retain. So why blame me?'

"When the weaver woke up, he peered into his bundle
and found that the gold coins had disappeared. He

began to think sadly, 'Oh, whatever has happened? I took so much time and trouble to earn this money and it has vanished in a moment. All my efforts were in vain. How can I show my face to my wife and friends in this poverty-stricken condition?'

"And so, he decided not to continue the journey home and he returned to Vardhamanapura.

"In a year's time, he had earned five hundred gold coins. Once more, he started off on his homeward journey. As before, half way home, he was still deep in the jungle when the sun set. For fear of losing his gold coins, as on the previous occasion, he did not stop to rest but continued to walk fast, even though he was very tired.

"After a while, he heard voices. Two men were talking:
—'Action!' said one of them to the other. 'Why did you let Somilaka earn five hundred gold pieces? Don't you know that he is destined to earn only what he requires for his food and clothing?'
—'Destiny!' replied the other. 'What could I do? The man put in a great effort and I had to reward him according to his actions. But it is still for you to decide how much he is going to retain. So why blame me?'

"When Somilaka heard this, he peered into his bag and found that the gold coins had disappeared.

"He was so utterly disheartened that he thought to himself, 'Oh, what is the good of living, if I have lost my money. I shall hang myself from this banyan tree.'

"And so, he wove a rope of grass, made a noose and tied the rope to the tree. He put the noose around his neck and was just about to throw himself down, when he heard a voice from heaven.

—'Somilaka!' said the voice. 'Stop! Don't do such a thing! It is I, Destiny, who stole your gold coins. I cannot bear that you should earn even a cowrie* more than what you require for your food and clothing. But I am pleased with your industrious spirit. I have not revealed myself to you in vain—ask any boon of me and I will

grant it.'
—'Very well then,' replied Somilaka, 'please give me a lot of money.'
—'But what will you do with money that you can't make use of?' asked the voice. 'You are not destined to earn more than what you require for your food and clothing.'
—'Even if I can't enjoy it,' said Somilaka, 'please give it to me, for:

"A man who has riches,

Is always well received by everyone,

Even if he is a miser or of low caste." '

—'Ah!' said the voice from the sky. 'But first return to Vardhamanapura and go to the homes of two merchants. One is called Guptadhana* and the other, Upabhukta-dhana*. When you have studied their behaviour, come back and tell me whether you would prefer to be like Guptadhana and have money but not enjoy it, or to be like Upabhuktadhana and have no surplus money because you enjoy spending all what you have.' Then the voice in the sky ceased.

"And so, Somilaka started back to Vardhamanapura in a dazed condition. By evening he reached the city, absolutely worn out. He inquired for Guptadhana's house and finally arrived there. Although Guptadhana, his wife and his son objected very strongly, he forcibly entered their house and became their guest.

"When it was meal time, they gave him food but in a most insulting manner. When he had finished eating, he went off to bed. While he slept, he heard the same two people talking:
—'Action!' said one of them to the other. 'Why did you force Guptadhana to provide Somilaka with a meal when he gave it so begrudgingly. Don't you know that Guptadhana is destined to have money but not enjoy spending it on himself or others?'
—'Destiny!' replied the other. 'What could I do? Somilaka's needs had to be provided for and Guptadhana did it according to his own miserly nature. But it is for

you to decide the final outcome. So why blame me?'

"Early the following morning, when Somilaka got up, he found that Guptadhana had an attack of cholera, and couldn't eat all day.

"Then Somilaka went on to Upabhuktadhana's house. He was welcomed with open arms. His hosts provided him with excellent bathing facilities and gave him new clothes. Afterwards he dined lavishly.

"At night time, he retired to a comfortable bed and went to sleep. While he slept, he heard the same two people talking:

—'Action!' said one of them to the other. 'Why did you allow Upabhuktadhana to entertain Somilaka so extravagantly, even to the extent of asking for credit at the grocer's? Don't you know that Upabhuktadhana is destined to have no surplus money because he enjoys spending all what he has?'

—'Destiny!' replied the other. 'What could I do? Somilaka's needs had to be provided for and Upabhuktadhana did it according to his own generous nature. But it is for you to decide the final outcome So why blame me?'

"Early next morning, one of the king's servants arrived and brought money for Upabhuktadhana.

"When Somilaka saw this, he said, 'This Upabhuktadhana is not a rich man and yet he is better off than Guptadhana. Let Destiny make me like Upabhuktadhana.'

"His wish was granted and he began to enjoy his money to the full just like Upabhuktadhana.

—"And so," continued Mantharaka, "that's why I said:
    'A wise man uses his wits
    To make money
    But avoids being a miser,
    For he may be destined to lose his money:
    The art is in learning how to enjoy it.
    This is what Somilaka learned in the deep jungle.'

—"Hiranyaka," continued Mantharaka, "knowing this,

one should not worry about riches. If someone has
riches and is unable to enjoy them, it's the same as if
he had nothing. It is true, what they say:
  'A man should use his money
  To provide for his necessities
  And to give to charity,
  But not to hoard,
  For the bees hoard their honey
  And people take it away.
  Even if he hoards it to give to others,
  It's still not a good thing,
  For it's like handling mud
  And then washing your hands.
  Contentment is what he should aim at,
  For this is the source of joy,
  But how can a greedy miser
  Ever understand the meaning of joy?
  Now, snakes can live on next to nothing
  And elephants eat only green stuff,
  Great sages live on nothing but fruits and herbs,
  But all these are strong,
  For they are content with what they have.
  But what will a man not do for money?
  He will cast a slur on the righteous,
  And praise the wicked.' "

When Mantharaka had finished speaking, the crow
turned to the mouse and said, "My friend, what
Mantharaka has said just now is very true and should
be put into practice. Don't mind his talking like this.
Only a real friend will say something unpalatable for
your own good, the rest are friends only in name."

While they were talking, a stag, by the name of
Chitranga*, turned up on the scene. He was in a state
of panic because the hunters were after him. When they
saw him coming, the crow flew up a tree, the mouse
slipped into the bushes and Mantharaka crawled into
the lake.

When the crow had been watching the stag carefully

for a short time, he called out to the turtle, "Mantharaka! Come out, it's all right. This stag has only come to quench his thirst."

But Mantharaka, who was a great observer of human nature, replied, "No, No, Laghupatanaka, I don't think this stag has come to drink water. He is panting for breath and looking fearfully over his shoulder. I think, he is being pursued by hunters. Go and find out whether I am right or not." So the crow flew off.

Then the stag said, "Turtle! You have understood why I am frightened. I escaped the hunter's arrow and have managed to get this far. Now, I beg of you, show me some place to hide, where the hunters can't reach me."

—"Stag," replied Mantharaka, "listen to the nitishastra:
'There are two ways of rescuing yourself
From the clutches of an enemy:
You can use your hands to fight
Or your feet to run.'

—"So in this case, before the wicked hunters arrive, run into the deep jungle over there." And he pointed out the direction.

Meanwhile, the crow, who had gone to see whether the hunters were about or not, returned and went after the stag. "Chitranga," he called, "it's alright! The wicked hunters have killed many animals and have gone with the carcasses. You can come out of the jungle."

And so, the four of them got friendly and, from that time onward, would meet everyday at noon, under the shady trees on the bank of the lake and discuss morals and philosophy. In this way, they spent their time very happily.

One day it was noon but Chitranga had failed to turn up. The other three got frightened and said to each other, "How is it that our friend has not come? Has he been killed by a lion or shot by the hunter's arrow or been burnt in a forest fire or caught in a trap? Or has he fallen in a deep pit whilst trying to reach fresh grass?"

Then Mantharaka said to the crow, "Laghupatanaka! Hiranyaka and I move slowly, so we can't possibly go looking for Chitranga, but you can fly fast. You had better go and search for him to see if he is alive or dead."

Laghupatanaka started off promptly, but he had flown only a short distance when he discovered Chitranga caught in a net on the bank of the lake. When the crow saw him, he was very upset and said to him, "My dear fellow! How did this happen?"

When the stag saw the crow, he too showed great distress and, with tears in his eyes, he said, "I am on the verge of death. I am very glad that you have found me before I die because I want to say to you that if I have ever, thoughtlessly, said or done anything unkind to you, please forgive me. And please say the same to Hiranyaka and Mantharaka on my behalf."

—"But, Chitranga!" said Laghupatanaka. "Please don't give up hope when you have friends like us. I shall hurry back and fetch Hiranyaka. Don't be afraid."

In this way, the crow put courage in the stag's heart and quickly flew to Hiranyaka and Mantharaka and told them about Chitranga's captivity. The mouse said he would rescue Chitranga and jumped on the crow's back. Then the two of them made their way swiftly to where Chitranga was.

When Chitranga saw them, his spirits brightened and he said:

"The wise choose good friends,
    For, with their help,
    It is possible to survive every calamity."

Then Hiranyaka said to Chitranga, "My friend, you know the nitishastras so well! How was it then that you got caught in this trap?"

—"Hiranyaka," replied Chitranga, "please, this isn't the time for discussion. Bite off these meshes and free me, before the hunter returns."

—"Now that I am here, you need not worry about the

hunter," said Hiranyaka, "but when people like you get caught in traps, whatever is the good of studying nitishastras!"

—"But, if fate is hostile," said Chitranga, "even your knowledge of nitishastras does not help you. As they say:

'When Destiny frowns on him,
Even a sage
May lose his power of thought.
What is predestined
Cannot be avoided
Even by the great.' "

While they were discussing this, Mantharaka, who was worried about his friend's welfare, also arrived on the scene.

When Laghupatanaka saw him coming, he said, "Oh. no! Look, Hiranyaka!"

—"What?" said Hiranyaka. "Is the hunter coming?"

—"Hunter—nothing!" retorted Laghupatanaka. "It's Mantharaka who is coming! How silly of him! If the hunter arrives, we shall all be in danger because of him for, I can easily fly away. You, Hiranyaka, can slip into a hole and Chitranga, when he is freed, can run. But what can this water dweller do to save himself? That's what worries me."

Meanwhile Mantharaka reached them. "Friend," said Hiranyaka, "you have done a silly thing in coming here! You had better go back as quickly as you can, before the hunter arrives."

—"But, Hiranyaka," said Mantharaka, "what else could I do? I couldn't bear to sit and think of my friend suffering, so I came here. I would rather lose my life than lose friends like you. We can get our lives back in the next birth, but not the friends we've lost."

While they were talking, the hunter appeared with an arrow fixed to his bow. As soon as they saw him approaching, Hiranyaka quickly finished biting off Chitranga's meshes and the stag bolted. Laghupatanaka

flew to the top of a tree and Hiranyaka slipped into a
hole near by.

The hunter was very disappointed to see the stag
escape, but when he saw Mantharaka slowly dragging
himself towards the lake, he thought to himself, "Fate
has snatched away the stag from me, but at least it has
sent this turtle for my food. His flesh will satisfy my
whole family."

And so, the hunter caught the turtle and tied him up
with a net of grass blades. And, slinging him on his
shoulder, beside his bow, he started off for home.

When Hiranyaka saw the turtle being carried away,
he was heart-broken and he said, "Oh, what a dreadful
thing to happen to us! Hardly had we got over one
trouble when the other was upon us! Disasters never
come singly. Destiny, that destroyed my hoard of food,
has also snatched away my friend, and a friend like
Mantharaka is not easy to find. Destiny, why are you
showering me with arrows of misfortune? First I lost
my hoard of food, then I was separated from my friends
and family, then I had to leave my home, and now, as
if all that wasn't enough, my dearest friend has been
snatched away from me for ever. Such is the fate of
all living creatures. They say:

'You get more cuts
Where there's already a wound,
And when the money is short,
You feel more hungry than usual!'
And,
'When you are already in trouble,
Your enemies multiply,
And when you are weak
Most evils arise.' "

Meanwhile, Laghupatanaka and Chitranga arrived
where Hiranyaka was, their eyes flooding with tears.
—"You can stop crying," said Hiranyaka, "and do
something about it before Mantharaka gets out of sight.
We must think of a plan to save him. As they say:

'When calamity strikes,
    To cry serves no purpose,
    It only increases the sorrow.' "
—"You are right," said the crow. "Listen, I have a plan.
Let Chitranga lie on the ground in the hunter's path
as though he was dead. I will sit on his head and
pretend to peck at his eyes with my beak. Then the
hunter will think, Chitranga is really dead and he will
drop Mantharaka and run after Chitranga. The minute
he does this, Hiranyaka must start biting the grass net
and set Mantharaka free. Mantharaka will then make
for the lake, as fast as he can. Meanwhile, Chitranga,
I shall tell you the right moment to get up and make
a dash to safety, before the hunter can reach you."
—"What an excellent plan!" said Chitranga. "I take it
for granted that Mantharaka is as good as free. As they
say:
    'A wise man's instinct tells him,
    If a plan is going to succeed or not.' "
And so they carried out Laghupatanaka's plan.

The hunter was going along the bank of the lake when
suddenly, he saw a stag lying in his path and a crow
pecking at his eyes. Delighted with the sight, he said,
"This is the same stag that slipped from my clutches
and escaped into the jungle. Perhaps he has died of
exhaustion. Well, the turtle is safely tied up, so I will
drop him and catch the stag. Then I shall have them
both."

And so, he put down the turtle and approached the
stag. In the meantime, Hiranyaka quickly bit the meshes
with his sharp teeth and Mantharaka crawled to the
safety of the lake. Chitranga, prompted by the crow,
also made a dash to safety and Hiranyaka and
Laghupatanaka also fled to safety.

The hunter looked dejectedly after the bolting stag
and then returned to the place where he had dropped
the turtle. He was astonished to find him gone. He
stood amazed and sadly addressed his fate in the

following words: "Destiny! A fat stag, that was caught in my net, was snatched away from me by you! A turtle vanished at your command. Here I am, wandering solitary and hungry in the jungle. If there is something else you want to do to me, then do it now! I am ready to bear it." After crying out in this way for some time, he finally went home.

When the hunter was gone, the four friends came out of the hiding places and danced with delight. They hugged each other joyfully and returned to their usual place, on the bank of the lake. They felt as though they had been reborn. From then on, they spent their time very happily, talking to each other about philosophy and morals.

And so, it is wise to make an effort to make friends and to behave straightforwardly towards them, for:

"He who makes friends
And never deceives them,
Shall triumph over all his troubles."

THE END
OF THE SECOND TANTRA

CROWS AND OWLS

This is the beginning of the third tantra, called "Crows and owls" and here is the first verse:

"Never trust a man
Who has always been your enemy
And suddenly turns friendly towards you.
This was the mistake the owls made
And the crows burnt them all alive in their cave."

This is how the story goes:

In the south of India, there was a city called Mahilaropyam. Not far from the city stood a huge banyan tree, with innumerable branches and leaves.

On this tree, lived Meghavarana*, king of the crows, and with him, his vast retinue.

Some way off, in a cave, lived Arimaradana*, king of the owls, and his court.

Now, the king of the owls regarded the crows as deadly enemies. Every night, the owls would fly round the vicinity of the banyan tree and kill any crow they could catch hold of. As a result, the crow's numbers began to dwindle rapidly. As they say:

"Suppress your enemy and diseases
At the very beginning,
Or they will become strong
And destroy you."

One day, Meghavarana, the crow king, called a council of his ministers and addressed them with these words, "Gentlemen, our enemy is dangerous and untiring. As he knows how to take advantage of a situation, that's why he always attacks at night. He succeeds in killing us in great numbers for, how can we possibly fight him off in the dark, when we are unable to see. On the other hand, during the daytime, we can't possibly attack him, because we don't know where the owl's stronghold is. So now, we must choose between the six Diplomatic

Methods:

> 'Peace, war, retreat, entrenchment,
> Seeking the help of allies or intrigue.'

—"Which one do we prefer? Think it over and let me know."

—"Your Majesty," they replied, "it's a good thing you have asked us to express our opinions, for:

> 'Only when a minister is specifically asked for his
>   opinion,
> Should he say what he honestly thinks
> And then it should make no difference
> Whether his opinion is palatable or not.
> For, if a minister is nothing but a flatterer,
> Then he is in reality not a minister but an enemy.'

—"And so, Your Majesty," they went on, "we should all discuss this problem in secret and come to a decision."

Now, the crow king had five ministers: Ujjeevi*, Sanjeevi*, Anujeevi*, Prajeevi* and Chiranjeevi*. First of all he turned to Ujjeevi and said to him, "Ujjeevi, my friend, what would you suggest we do, as things stand?"

—"Your Majesty," he replied, "Arimaradana, the owl king, is strong and attacks at the right time. And so we should not fight him, for, Brihaspati has said:

> 'Make peace with an enemy
> Who is as strong as you are,
> For, in a battle between equals,
> The victory hangs in the balance,
> Never fight
> Unless you are sure of success.' "

—Ujjeevi advised the king to make peace.

Then the king turned to Sanjeevi and said to him, "Sanjeevi, my friend, I should like to hear your opinion."

—"Your Majesty," he replied, "Arimaradana, the owl king, is cruel and he has no ethics. Peace with someone like that cannot last long. I suggest that we do fight him. They say:

> 'If a weak man is full of fire,

He can destroy an enemy who is stronger,
Just as a lion kills an elephant
And rules over his domain.' "
—Sanjeevi advised the king to go to war.

Then the king turned to Anujeevi and said to him,
"Anujeevi, my friend, you too express your viewpoint."
—"Your Majesty," he replied, "Arimaradana, the owl
king, is stronger than we are, so we cannot fight him.
He is also cruel and without ethics, so we cannot make
peace with him, for such peace won't last long. So, I
suggest that we retreat. As they say:

'A ram retreats to attack
And a lion crouches to pounce on his prey.' "
—Anujeevi advised the king to retreat.

Then the king turned to Prajeevi and said to him,
"Prajeevi, my friend, what do you think?"
—"Your Majesty," he replied, "in my opinion, these
three suggestions, peace, war and retreat, are useless. I
think entrenchment is the right course of action. For
they say:

'A crocodile in water
Can drag an elephant
But outside, on land,
He is harassed by a mere dog.'
And,
'A single archer, well entrenched,
Can withstand a hundred men of the enemy.'
But,
'He who, in the face of a strong enemy,
Instead of entrenching himself,
Deserts his post,
Shall never see it again.'
—"And so, entrenchment is the right course of action.."
—Prajeevi advised the king for entrenchment.

Then Meghavarana turned to Chiranjeevi and said to
him, "Chiranjeevi, my friend, what do you think?"
—"Your Majesty," he replied, "in my opinion, seeking
the help of the allies is the only answer. For they say:

'Blazing fire, without the help of the wind,
    Will go out.'
—"So we should seek assistance, preferably from
someone very strong, but even a group of lesser people
would do."
—Chiranjeevi advised the king to seek the help of allies.
    Finally, the crow king turned to Sthirajeevi*, his father's
old minister, and said to him, "Tata*, I have asked all
these ministers for their opinions in your presence,
merely for the sake of putting them to the test. Now
that you have heard them all, kindly tell me the right
course for us to adopt."
—"Your Majesty," he replied, "all these ministers have
expressed their views in accordance with the nitishastra
and the courses of action they recommend, will indeed
give good results, but under different circumstances.
However, in the present case, we should use intrigue,
for they say:
    'Only intrigue is effectual
    When your enemy is powerful.'
And,
    'Just as guda* first increases the mucous
    And afterwards suppresses it,
    So the wise first puff up the enemy
    And afterwards destroy them.'
—"Now, what you must do, is find out your enemy's
weak points and then take advantage of them at the
opportune time."
—"How can I know his weak points," said the king,
"when I am not even aware of where he lives and have
no contact whatsoever with him?"
—"Through spies!" replied Sthirajeevi. "They say:
    'Animals are guided by their sense of smell,
    Brahmins through the Vedas,
    Kings through spies
    And other men by their two eyes.' "
    When Meghavarana had heard this advice, he said to
Sthirajeevi, "But tell me, Tata, why this deadly enmity

between crows and owls? There must be some good reason for it."

And, by way of reply, Sthirajeevi told:

THE STORY OF THE ENMITY BETWEEN
CROWS AND OWLS

"Once upon a time, all the birds, the swans, the parrots, cranes, cuckoos, nightingales, owls, peacocks, doves, partridges and the rest of them, had a meeting. They began to hold a discussion with great vehemence.

—'Garuda is our king,' they said, 'but he is so busy serving Lord Vishnu, that he doesn't bother about us. What is the point of having a master who is just a namesake! He never helps us to get out of the traps set by hunters! They say:

"As a boat without a helmsman
Just drifts with the tide,
So too the people come to grief,
When their king takes no care of them.
So never put your faith in such a king
Any more than you would in a sinking ship in the
   ocean.

The same applies to:
A teacher who does not teach,
A Brahmin who does not study the Vedas*,
A wife who has a sharp tongue,
A cowherd in a town
And a barber who wants to become a Sanyasi."

—'And so,' continued the birds, 'let us consider the matter carefully and elect a new king!'

"Now when the birds looked round at one another, they noticed that the owl had very impressive features and everyone said, 'The owl shall be our king. Bring the things that are necessary for the coronation!'

"And so, the birds collected water from the holy rivers and also a hundred and eight different roots. The throne was decorated lavishly and a tiger skin was spread over the ground in front of it. They drew a map of all the continents and the oceans. They beat the drums and blew the conches. Brahmins began to recite the Vedas and beautiful maidens sang songs of joy.

"But just as the owl was being led to the throne to be crowned, a crow arrived on the scene and demanded, 'What is the meaning of this great gathering of birds?'

"When the birds saw the crow, they said to one another, 'Let's have his opinion too, for they say:

"A barber is the shrewdest amongst men,
A crow amongst birds,
A jackal amongst animals,
And a white-robed Jain Muni* amongst hermits."
And,
"A plan, once decided upon,
In consultation with a wise man,
Will never go astray." '

—'Birds,' repeated the crow, 'why this meeting and why this celebration?'

—'Friend,' replied the birds, 'we birds have no king of our own, and so we have decided to crown this owl as our king. You have come just in time to give us your opinion too.'

—'Well,' replied the crow with a smile, 'my advice is against crowning the owl our king. Why choose this ugly and blind-by-day owl, when we have amongst us the best of the birds—peacocks, swans, cuckoos, nightingales, pigeons, cranes, and so on! I certainly advise against it! His crooked nose and his squint eyes make him look cruel, even when he is not angry. Whatever would he look like if he was really angry? What could we possibly gain by electing such an ugly and vicious-looking leader. And what is more, even if this owl has his qualities, it is not necessary to elect another king. We already have Garuda, and just by mentioning his name, you can keep your enemies at bay. They say:

"The mere utterance of a great man's name
Helps you get out of difficulties.
In this way, the hares mentioned the name of
Chandrama*

And lived happily ever after." '
—'How was that?' asked the birds.
And the crow told:

THE STORY OF THE HARES AND THE ELEPHANTS

" 'In a certain place, there lived an elephant king and with him, his retinue. The king's name was Chaturadanta*.

" 'Once there was no rain for a good many years and the lakes and ponds all dried up. The elephants went to their king and said to him, "Your Majesty! Parched by thirst, some of our little ones have already died, whilst the rest of them are on the verge of death. We must find some place where we can drink as much water as we want to."

" 'After deep reflection, their leader replied, "I know a place where there is a big lake which is always full, because it is fed by an underground water supply. We'll go there."

" 'And so the elephants marched five days and five nights, and early the following morning, reached the lake.

" 'Now, in the soft earth, around the lake, there were innumerable holes, the homes of the hares. When the elephants plunged jubilantly into the water, these holes were destroyed and many hares were trampled underneath. Quite a few died, whilst there were others who were seriously injured.

" 'When the elephants had left the lake, the surviving hares assembled, crying pitifully, "Oh, dear, dear, dear! Because water is not to be had anywhere else, these elephants are bound to come here everyday and trample on us. We must think what to do."

" 'Then one of them said, "What else can we do but leave this place?"

" 'But the other hares replied, "What, friend! Give up our ancestral home so suddenly! It's impossible! No, we must frighten the elephants so much that they never think of coming back. We are only hares but still we are capable of it."

" 'Then one of them said, "I know a way to frighten them off but we will need a very clever diplomat who is good at pretending. My plan is this: This fellow approaches the elephant king and says that he has been sent by Chandrama. He tells him that Chandrama forbids the elephants to come to the lake, because it's the home of the hares, his people. Now, if the elephant king is taken in by this story, he will go away."

—"Well," said another hare, "we have, amongst us, Lambakarana* who is very clever and an excellent talker. We can send him, for they say:

'A messenger should be someone
Who has wits, good looks and an unselfish nature,
An excellent conversationalist, with a thorough
    knowledge of the shastras,
Someone who understands the minds of other
    people.' "

" 'Then the other hares said, "You are right! We will carry out your plan. There seems to be no other way of saving our lives."

" 'And so, Lambakarana was sent to the elephant king. After he had walked some way from the lake, he came across a hillock which lay in the path of the elephants, but was too high for them to reach. He sat down on it. When the elephant king passed by with his herd, the hare cried out to him, threateningly, "Hey, you! Wicked elephant! Don't you dare approach this lake! It belongs to Chandrama. Go back!"

" 'The elephant king was taken by surprise and said to the hare, "Who are you?"

—"My name is Lambakarana," replied the hare, "and I am Chandrama's messenger. He has sent me to you!"

—"Hare!" said the elephant king. "Tell me his message immediately and we will obey him!"

—"The message is this," said Lambakarana. "If you want to stay alive, don't ever return to this lake again. For, yesterday you visited the lake and trampled on innumerable hares, who are under my protection."

—"I see," replied the elephant king. "Well, where is Lord Chandrama now?"

—"He has come down to the lake himself to console the surviving hares," said Lambakarana.

—"Then lead me to him," said the elephant king, "so that I can beg his forgiveness and then go away."

—"All right then," said Lambakarana, "come along with me."

" 'By now, it was evening. The hare took the elephant king to the bank of the lake and showed him the reflection of the moon in the water.

—"Our Master is sitting in deep meditation," he said. "Bow to him silently and leave, for if you disturb him while he is meditating, he will be furious with you!"

" 'Accordingly, the elephant bowed from a distance and went away trembling. And from that day onward, the hares lived happily ever after.

—'And so,' continued the crow, 'that's why I said:

"The mere utterance of a great man's name
Helps you get out of difficulties.
The hares mentioned the name of Chandrama
And lived happily ever after."

—'And another thing, if you want to stay alive, don't elect a sly and vicious king. As they say:

"The hare and the partridge were destroyed
Because they chose a sly and vicious arbitrator." '

—'How was that?' asked the birds.

And the crow told:

THE STORY OF THE HARE AND THE PARTRIDGE

" 'Once upon a time, I was living in a certain tree. In the hollow, at the foot of the tree, lived a partridge, by the name of Kapinjala*. In the course of time, we became good friends. Every day, at sunset, we would return home and tell each other stories about Rishis* and such things, and talk over together what had happened during the day. In this way, we passed our time very contentedly.

" 'One day, Kapinjala went off, with some other partridges, to another part of the country, which was full of ripe rice. When he did not return at nightfall, I became very worried and thought to myself, "Oh dear, why hasn't Kapinjala returned home today? Has he been caught in a trap or has somebody killed him? I am sure he would have returned if he was safe, for he can't live without me!"

" 'And so, I spent several days worrying.

" 'One day, at nightfall, a hare, by the name of Sheeghraga*, came and took over the hole in the tree. As I had given up all hope of ever seeing Kapinjala again, I did not object in any way to his occupying the place.

" 'Meanwhile, Kapinjala, who had become fat from eating the ripe rice, suddenly remembered his former home and came back. When he found the hare living in his house, he objected very strongly and said to him, "Hare! You have taken my home! That's very unfair of you! Leave immediately!"

—"Oh, but this place is mine now," said the hare, "for they say:

'A well, a pond, a temple and a tree,
    Once given up by their owners,
    Cannot be reclaimed.'

—"Now, this precept, enjoined by the sages for human beings, is also applicable to birds and animals. So this place is mine and not yours."

—"Hare!" said Kapinjala. "If you are quoting the shastras, then let us approach someone who is well versed in them and we'll let him decide who is to have the place."

" 'Both agreed to this suggestion and set off together to have their dispute decided by a Shastri*.

—'Out of curiosity,' continued the crow, 'I followed them, thinking to myself, "I would very much like to hear the decision in this case!" '

" 'Now, a wild tomcat, by the name of Teekshadaunstra*, came to know about their dispute. He went and stood in their path, on the bank of the river. In his paw he held a blade of Kusha grass*. He closed his eyes, stood on his hind legs, facing the sun, and began giving a discourse on morals.

—"Ah! Life is transitory and this world is futile. The company of loved ones is nothing but a dream and the presence of the family like the trick of a conjurer. They say:

'Our bodies are perishable
And even our money does not last for ever,
We face death continually,
So we must live according to the shastras.
A man who passes his days irreligiously,
Is like an ironsmith's bellows
Which breathes, yet has no life.'

—"Why make a long story of it? I'll tell you what religion is, in a nutshell. To do good to others is virtuous but harming others is a sin."

" 'When the hare heard this religious discourse, he said to the partridge, "Kapinjala! This fellow, sitting on the bank of the river, is a Tapasvi* and an exponent of religion. Let us go and ask his opinion."

—"All right," said Kapinjala, "but he is a wild tomcat and our natural enemy, so we should talk to him from a very long way off."

" 'And so, standing at a distance, they both said to

him, "Tapasvi! There is a dispute between us. Give us your opinion, in accordance with the shastras, and whichever of us is in the wrong, you can eat up."

—"My friends," said the tomcat, "please don't talk like that! I have given up that violent way of life which leads directly to hell. The sages have declared non-violence to be the essence of true religion. It's wrong to kill even lice, bugs and mosquitoes, so I shall certainly not kill you. However, I will decide who wins and who loses in this dispute. But I am old and I can't hear what it's all about from so far away. So come nearer and present your case, so that I can decide in such a way, that I am not held blameworthy in the next world, for they say:

'He who arbitrates unjustly,

Out of pride, avarice, anger or fear,

Shall surely go to hell.'

—"So, have confidence in me and speak the facts clearly in my ears. What more is there for me to say?"

" 'And so, this wicked tomcat inspired so much confidence in the partridge and the hare, that they came and sat close to him. Immediately, he seized one of them in his teeth and the other in his claws, killed them both and ate them up.

—'And so,' continued the crow, 'that's why I said,

"The hare and the partridge were destroyed

Because they chose a sly and vicious arbitrator."

—'Now, if you choose this blind-by-day owl to be your king, you are following the path of the hare and the partridge. Realise this and act accordingly.'

"When the birds heard the crow, they said to one another, 'He is right. We'll meet some other time and select another king.' And then they all flew off, except the crow, the owl and the owl's wife, Krikalika*.

"The owl was still waiting to be crowned king. He turned to his wife and said, 'What is all this? Why hasn't the ceremony to crown me begun yet?'

—'This crow has put an obstacle in the way of your

being crowned,' said his wife. 'All the other birds have
flown away, only this crow has stayed behind, for some
reason. And so we had better go home too.'

"When the owl heard this, he was disappointed and
said to the crow, "Wicked crow! What harm have I
done you, that you should put obstacles in the way of
my being crowned king. From now on there shall be
enmity between you and me, and between your kind
and my kind, for they say:

"The wound caused by an arrow or a sword may
    heal,
But not the wound caused by sharp words." '

"With these words, the owl returned to his place, with
his wife.

"When they had gone, the crow thought to himself,
'Whyever did I talk like that and pick up a quarrel with
the owl? They say:

"A wise man, even if he is very strong,
Never makes enemies for himself."

And,

"No wise man should speak ill of others
In an assembly, even if it is the truth,
For it may lead to his own downfall." '

"With this thought, the crow too went home.

—"And that, Your Majesty," continued Sthirajeevi, the
'd minister, "is the reason why, ever since, there has
be   enmity between crows and owls."

Then Meghavarana, the crow king, said to him, "Tata,
as this is how things stand, what should we do?"

—"Your Majesty," replied Sthirajeevi, "intrigue is the
only thing that will work. I mean to use this method
personally and so destroy the enemy. As they say:

'Through intrigue, three shrewd crooks
Robbed a Brahmin of his goat.' "

—"How was that?" asked Meghavarana.
And Sthirajeevi told:

THE STORY OF THE BRAHMIN AND
THE THREE CROOKS

"In a certain town, there lived a Brahmin, by the name of Mitra Sharma*, who was a fire worshipper.

"One day, in the month of Magha*, a gentle breeze was blowing and the sky was overcast with clouds. The Brahmin set out for another village, to visit a certain devotee, so that he could beg a goat for sacrifice.

"When he arrived there, he said to his devotee, 'My son, on the coming of Amavasya*, I want to perform a sacrifice, so please make me a present of some fat animal.' His devotee agreed and gave him a fat goat. The Brahmin put him on his shoulder, so that he shouldn't run away, and started the return journey.

"On his way home, he was seen by three crooks, who were almost starving. They said to one another, 'If we could only lay hands on this fat goat, we wouldn't have to suffer from cold and hunger. So, let's play a trick on the Brahmin and make him part with him.'

"Then the first crook disguised himself, went ahead of the Brahmin by a side road and stood in his path. When the Brahmin approached, he cried, 'Ho! Fire worshipper! Why are you behaving so ridiculously? Why are you carrying this profane dog on your shoulders?'

"The Brahmin got excited and cried, 'Are you blind that you call this sacrificial goat a dog?'

And the crook replied, 'Please don't get cross. Have it your own way and do as you please.'

"When the Brahmin had gone a little further, the second crook accosted him and said, 'Ho! Brahmin! Shame on you, shame! Even if this dead calf was very dear to you, you shouldn't carry him about on your shoulders like that.'

"The Brahmin replied in great anger, 'Are you blind that you call this living goat a dead calf?'

And the crook replied, 'Please don't get cross. My

mistake for talking to you! Have it your own way and do as you please.'

"When the Brahmin had gone still a little further, the third crook appeared on the scene and said, 'Ho! Brahmin! It's highly improper for you to carry a donkey on your shoulders. Drop him quickly, before anyone sees you!'

"Now, after all this, the Brahmin thought that he must really be carrying a goblin, which was changing shape all the while. He threw him off on the ground, and, terrified, ran home.

"The three crooks caught hold of the goat, killed him and ate him up to their heart's content.

—"And so," continued Sthirajeevi, "that's why I said,

'Through intrigue, three shrewd crooks
Robbed a Brahmin of his goat.'

—"In just the same way, a clever and tricky person can outwit a strong enemy. As they say:

'Most people are taken in by
The intriguing talk of a rogue,
The pretended politeness of a new servant,
The charming conversation of guests
And a woman's false tears.'

—"Now, I shall unfold my plan as to how we can outwit and destroy the enemy. Listen carefully."

—"Please tell me," said Meghavarana, "and I shall follow your advice."

—"Well," said Sthirajeevi, "pretend that I am your enemy. Curse me with cruel words, spatter me with blood and throw me at the foot of the banyan tree, so that the enemy spies are misled into thinking that it is you who have reduced me to this condition. Then, fly with your entire family and court to Rshyamukam* Mountain. Entrench yourself there, until I can inspire confidence in the enemy. I shall make a thorough investigation of their stronghold and afterwards, we shall burn the owls during the daytime, for it's then that they are blind and will be unable to escape. Now, please

don't be afraid of me and put obstacles in my way."
—"Very well then," replied the king. "I agree."

And so, Sthirajeevi started a sham quarrel with Meghavarana. When the crow king's followers heard Sthirajeevi's abusive language, they were ready to kill him, but Meghavarana restrained them and said, "Away! I'll take care of this enemy agent personally." Then he pounced upon Sthirajeevi and began to peck him with his beak. He smeared him with the blood of a dead animal and left him lying at the foot of the banyan tree. Then he flew away with his court.

Now, the wife of the owl king happened to be spying at that time. She went and reported to her husband, "Your enemy is in a state of panic. He has flown off with his court." When the owl king heard this, he waited for sunset and then set out with his retinue and the rest of the owls to look for the crows and kill them. "Hurry up!" he cried. "It's good luck to have a terrified enemy!"

And so, all the owls flew to the banyan tree to be sure that the enemy had really left, and surrounded it from all sides. When they failed to find the crows, Arimaradana, the king of the owls, perched himself on a branch of the tree. His court gathered round him and started flattering him on his success, but he said, "Enough! Find out which way the enemy went. We must overtake them and kill them before they entrench themselves!"

Meanwhile, Sthirajeevi had hidden himself at a vantage point. He thought to himself, "Now, whatever I have started, I must see through to the end, for they say:

'A wise man never begins
What he cannot bring to fruition.'

—"I think now is the moment for my next move. I shall make them aware of my presence."

And so, he began to caw feebly. Immediately, all the owls converged on him to kill him. "Stop!" cried the crow. "Listen to me! I am Sthirajeevi, the crow king

Meghavarana's minister. It is he who has reduced me
to this plight. Communicate this to your master. And
tell him that I have some particularly interesting
information to give him."

When the owl king heard this, he was very surprised.
He hurried to Sthirajeevi and said, "Good Gracious!
How did you come to be in this state! Tell me."

—"My Lord," replied Sthirajeevi, "this is how it
happened. Yesterday, when Meghavarana saw so many
of his crows killed by you, he got very excited and was
preparing to attack you, but I said to him, 'Master! It's
not wise to attack them, for they are strong and we are
weak. They say:

"A weak man, with his own interests at heart,
    Never dreams of provoking his enemy." '

—"What is more," continued Sthirajeevi, "I advised
Meghavarana to make peace with you, by offering
presents, for they say:

'When you encounter an enemy much stronger than
    you are,
To save your skin, hand everything over,
For money and possessions are easily regained,
But your life, once lost, you can never recover.'

—"But, Your Majesty, the other crows incited
Meghavarana against me and they are responsible for
my present condition. They did this because they
suspected me of being on your side. And so, now I
look to you for protection. What more is there for me
to say? As soon as I am able to fly again, I shall lead
you to where they are and you can kill them."

When Arimaradana heard this, he took counsel with
his five hereditary ministers. Their names were
Raktaksha*, Kruraksha*, Deeptaksha*, Vakranasa*, and
Prakarakarna*.

First of all, he turned to Raktaksha and said to him,
"My friend, my enemy's minister has fallen into my
hands. What shall I do with him?"

—"My Lord," he replied, "what else can we do? Kill

him at once without any hesitation. They say:

'Destroy an enemy
Before he becomes too powerful to be defeated.'

—"And now to kill him is easy. But if you don't take advantage of this opportunity, you may not have such a chance again, even if you desire it. And, don't be taken in by his pretence of friendship. He is our enemy! As the cobra said:

'Look at the funeral pyre
And then at my injured hood.
Love, once shattered,
Can never be restored by a show of affection.' "

—"How was that?" asked Arimaradana.

And Raktaksha told:

THE STORY OF THE BRAHMIN AND THE COBRA

"In a certain town, there lived a Brahmin, by the name of Haridatta*. In spite of the fact that he worked extremely hard on his farm, he did not prosper.

"One day, the heat was unbearable and he was resting under the shade of a tree, on the farm, when a cobra emerged from an ant-hill and confronted him, his hood raised.

"He thought to himself, 'Perhaps this cobra is the deity of the farm. As I have not worshipped him before, my labour on the farm has proved to be fruitless. So, from today onwards, I shall start offering oblations to him.'

"With this thought, the Brahmin brought milk and poured into a plate in front of the ant-hill and said, 'Oh, protector of the farm, I did not know of your presence here, that is why I have not worshipped you until now. Please forgive me.'

"And when he had offered the milk to the cobra, in the traditional way, he went home.

"Next morning, when he returned, he saw a gold coin lying on the plate.

"In this way, everyday the Brahmin would make an offering of milk to the cobra and get a gold coin in return.

"One day, the Brahmin went to visit another village, after duly instructing his son to make an offering of milk to the cobra. Accordingly, the following day, his son did so and then went home. Next morning, when he returned, he found a gold coin lying on the plate. He was astonished and thought to himself, 'This ant-hill must be full of gold coins. I'll kill the cobra and get all the gold at once.'

"And so, the morning after, when he should have been making an offering of milk, the Brahmin's son hit the cobra with a stick. But, luckily for the cobra, it was not a death blow and the cobra turned angrily on the Brahmin's son and bit him. The boy died on the spot and the Brahmin's relatives burnt his body in the field.

"Next day, when the Brahmin returned, his relatives informed him of his son's death and described to him the way he had died. The Brahmin expressed his grief for his son's rash behaviour and subsequent death but defended the cobra's action.

"The following morning the Brahmin went to the cobra with an offering of milk, stood before the ant-hill and prayed in a loud voice. The cobra, sitting at the entrance of the ant-hill, said, 'Good heavens! You're so greedy for gold that you have even forgotten your son's death to come here! Our friendship will not last long now. Your son, in his youthful rashness, attacked me and I, in retaliation, bit him. How can I forget your son's attack, and how can you forget his death? Look at the funeral pyre and then at my injured hood. Love, once shattered, can never be restored by a show of affection.'

"When the cobra had said this, he handed to the Brahmin a priceless diamond and re-entered the ant-hill, saying, 'Never come here again!'

"The Brahmin accepted the diamond, and went home, regretting his son's foolishness.

—"And so," continued Raktaksha, "that's why I said:

'Love, once shattered,

Can never be restored by a show of affection.'

—"That is why we should kill the crow and remove a potential danger to our kingdom."

When Arimaradana, the king of the owls, had heard Raktaksha's advice, he turned to Kruraksha and said, "My dear fellow, what do you have to say about this?"

—"My Lord," he replied, "what Raktaksha says is very cruel. We should not kill someone who has come to us for protection, for they say:

'A dove entertained an enemy

Who came to him for protection

And even went so far
    As to give his own flesh to him to eat.' "
—"How was that?" asked Arimaradana.
And Kruraksha told:

THE STORY OF THE DOVE AND THE HUNTER

"A wicked bird hunter, with the appearance of Yama, used to roam about in the jungle. He had neither friends nor relatives. He was deserted by everyone because of his cruel deeds. As they say:

'Wicked people who destroy life,
Are dangerous to be near.
They can well be compared to snakes
Who bite one and all.'

"One day, while the hunter was wandering about in the jungle, he caught a female dove and threw her into a cage.

"It was now evening. Suddenly, a storm, accompanied by heavy rain, broke loose, so ferociously that it seemed as if Pralaya* was at hand. The hunter was terrified and began to shudder from the rain and cold. He searched for somewhere to shelter and went and stood under a tree.

"After some time, however, the sky cleared and when the hunter looked up, he saw a bright star. Then he said in a loud voice, 'I seek shelter from whoever may be living in this tree. Let him protect me! I am bewildered by cold and hunger.'

"Now a pair of doves had, for a long time, made their nest in this tree. This particular evening, the female dove had not come home and her husband was desperately worried about her. 'The wind blows fiercely along with the rain,' he said, 'and my wife has not yet returned. My home is empty without her. As they say:

"A house without a wife
Cannot be called a home,
It's a desert." '

"Now the bird hunter had caught this very dove's wife and put her in his cage. When the trapped dove heard her husband talking like this, she replied to him,

'A wife whose husband is not pleased with her,

Cannot be called a wife,
But a woman who makes her husband happy,
Wins the esteem of the gods.
Now, a father, a brother and a son,
Give within limits,
But what wife won't desire to please her husband,
When he gives beyond limit.'

—'Now, my dear,' she went on, 'I want to tell you
something for your own good. Please listen. If someone
comes to you for shelter, he should be protected, even
if it means risking your own life. This hunter is cold
and hungry and he asks you to protect him. So, make
him welcome, for they say:

"Whoever does not welcome a guest, according to
his mite,
Will pay for all the sins of the guest
And lose to him all the fruits of his good deeds."

—'And don't hate this hunter because he has caged
your beloved. I have been imprisoned only as a result
of my past actions. Poverty, disease, grief, imprisonment
and disaster, all these come from one's own deeds. So,
stop hating the hunter because of my captivity, think
of religion ánd welcome him according to our traditions.'

"When the male dove heard his wife's virtuous words,
he approached the hunter warmly and said to him, 'My
friend, welcome! Consider this as your own home and
don't let anything worry you.'

"When the hunter heard this, he replied, 'Oh, dove!
Please protect me from this terrible cold.'

"The dove flew to a place some way off and brought
back a live coal. He dropped it on some dry leaves and
the flames began to spread rapidly. He said to the
hunter, 'Warm yourself and don't be afraid. But
unfortunately, I have nothing here to satisfy your
hunger. Some people entertain thousands, some
hundreds, some tens, but I am so wretched that I cannot
even support myself. But what is the good of staying
in the house of someone who is so beset with troubles

that he is unable to feed even one guest? So, what I shall do is sacrifice this sorrowful body of mine and make myself useful, then I shall not have to admit that I turned a guest away hungry from my door.'

"And so, the dove put all the blame on himself and said not a word of reproach to the hunter. Then he said, 'Just wait a moment, soon I shall satisfy your hunger.' When he had said this, with joy in his heart, the pious bird flew once round the fire and then entered it, as if it had been his own nest.

"When the hunter saw all this, his heart was moved with pity and he said, 'The mind of a man who lives wickedly is always in turmoil and ultimately he has to pay for his evil actions. I, as a result of all my sins, will undoubtedly go to hell. But this virtuous dove has set an ideal before me. From today on, I shall give up all my pleasures and lead a life of discipline.'

"And so the hunter threw away his net, released the unfortunate female dove and broke the cage into pieces.

"When the female dove saw her husband burnt in the fire, she began to wail and sob pitifully. 'Oh, My Lord!' she cried. 'What is the good of living without you? Widowhood results in loss of pride, loss of respect in the household and loss of authority over servants.'

"And so, heart-broken and crying pitifully, the devoted wife flew into the very same flames.

"Some time after her earthly death, the female dove saw her husband transformed into a divine creature. He was riding a chariot and wearing costly ornaments. The female dove found that she too had assumed a divine form and she went to her husband. 'My virtuous wife,' said the male dove, 'you have done well in following me.'

"And, as for the hunter, he renounced everything and began to live in the forest as a Tapasvi. His mind became free of all desires. One day, he saw a forest fire in front of him. He walked into it and his body was burnt. Thus he paid for his sins and entered heaven with great joy.

—"And so," continued Kruraksha, "that's why I said,

'A dove entertained an enemy
Who came to him for protection
And even went so far
As to give his own flesh to him to eat.' "

When Arimaradana, the owl king, had heard
Kruraksha's advice, he turned to Deeptaksha and asked
him, "My dear fellow, what would you advise, under
the circumstances?"

—"My Lord," he replied. "this crow should not be killed,
for he may prove beneficial to us by exposing the
weaknesses of his own clan. As they say:

'Even a thief proved beneficial
To an old man!' "

—"How was that?" asked Arimaradana.

And Deeptaksha told:

THE STORY OF THE OLD MERCHANT, HIS YOUNG WIFE AND THE THIEF

"In a certain town, there lived an old merchant, by the name of Kamatura*. After the death of his wife, he became so love-sick that he gave a lot of money to another merchant, so that he could marry his young daughter. However, his new wife was very unhappy and would not even look at her old husband. This is quite understandable, as they say:

'Young girls reject a man whose hair have turned grey,
They shrink from a limp and bent body.'

"Now, one night, as the young wife was lying in bed with her face turned away from her husband, a thief crept into the house. The girl was so terrified when she saw him that she turned and clasped her husband fervently. The old man was delighted beyond words but thought to himself, 'I wonder how it is that she is hugging me so tight.' He was peering cautiously about the room when he caught sight of the thief in the corner. Then he realised that she was hugging him because she was afraid of the thief. He cried out to the thief, 'My benefactor! Thank you! This woman was avoiding me but today she is hugging me lovingly in her arms! My good fellow, take away whatever you want!'

—'Well,' replied the thief, 'I can't see anything here worth stealing at the moment but I'll come back some other time to try my luck and to oblige you, in case your wife does not continue to behave lovingly towards you.

—"And so," continued Deeptaksha, "that's why I said, 'even a thief proved beneficial to an old man.' So why shouldn't this crow, who is seeking protection, be beneficial to us? The other crows have treated him badly, so he will certainly tell us their weak points.

Under no circumstances should he be killed."

When Arimaradana had heard Deeptaksha's advice, he turned to Vakranasa and said to him, "My dear fellow, what would you suggest under the circumstances?"
—"My Lord," he replied, "this crow should not be killed, for they say:

'If discord arises between your enemies,
You stand to benefit:
In the same way, the thief and the Rakshasa*
quarrelled
And the Brahmin saved his life and his calves as well.' "
—"How was that?" asked Arimaradana.
And Vakranasa told:

THE STORY OF THE BRAHMIN, THE THIEF AND THE RAKSHASA

"In a certain town, lived a Brahmin named Drona*. He gave up wearing fine clothes, using perfumes and all the other luxuries of life. His hair and nails grew long and his body lean, due to rigorous discipline in the cold, hot and rainy seasons.

"A certain devotee of his, out of sheer pity, presented him with a pair of young calves. Right from the beginning, he fed them on butter, oil and grain, and they grew fat.

"A thief saw these two calves and he thought to himself, 'This very day, I shall steal away these two calves belonging to the Brahim.' So he took a rope to tie them up and started off.

"On the way, he met a Rakshasa of hideous appearance. His teeth stuck out of his mouth, his nose was long, his eyes burnt frighteningly with fire, he had knotty muscles and a glowing red beard.

"When the thief saw him, he got frightened and said, 'Who are you?'

—'I am a Rakshasa called Satyavachana*,' replied the Rakshasa. 'Now you too introduce yourself.'

—'I'm a thief called Krurakarma*,' replied the thief, 'and I am on my way to steal two calves from a poor Brahmin.'

"Because both spoke the truth, the two of them developed faith in each other. The Rakshasa said to the thief, 'I'm extremely hungry today, I think I shall eat that Brahmin. As you are going to steal his calves, it's a very good thing, for our work will be accomplished at the same place.' And so they started off together. When they reached the Brahmin's home, they slipped inside and hid themselves, waiting for an opportune moment.

"When the Brahmin fell asleep, the Rakshasa got ready

to eat him but the thief restrained him and said, 'That's not fair! You have to wait until I have taken the calves! Otherwise, if he wakes up when you are about to eat him, my object will be defeated.'

—'On the contrary,' retorted the Rakshasa, 'if the calves cry out when you are leading them away and the Brahmin wakes up, I shall be the loser!'

"Because of the hot argument that developed between the two, the Brahmin did wake up. Then, the thief said to the Brahmin, 'Brahmin, this Rakshasa wants to eat you.'

And the Rakshasa said, 'Brahmin, this thief wants to steal your calves.'

"Now, the Brahmin became very wide awake and prayed to his chosen deity, whereupon the Rakshasa ran off. The Brahmin picked up a stick and chased the thief away.

—"And so," continued Vakranasa, "that's why I said,

'If discord arises between your enemies,
You stand to benefit:
In the same way, the thief and the Rakshasa quarrelled
And the Brahmin saved his life and his calves as well.' "

When Arimaradana heard what Vakranasa had to say, he turned to Prakarakarna and asked him, "Tell me, what is your point of view?"

—"My Lord," he replied, "this crow should not be killed. Perhaps a friendship will develop between him and us and we shall live very happily together, for they say:

'Those who refuse to co-operate,
Shall be destroyed like the two snakes.' "

—"How was that?" asked Arimaradana.

And Prakarakarna told:

THE STORY OF THE SNAKE IN THE ANT-HILL AND THE SNAKE IN THE BELLY OF THE PRINCE

"In a certain town, there lived a king, by the name of Devashakti*. He had a son who grew leaner and leaner everyday, for he had a snake in his stomach. In spite of several treatments by well-known physicians, he was not cured at all. Thoroughly fed up with his life, the prince went to another town, where he lived in a temple and maintained himself by begging alms.

"Now the king of that country had two young daughters. Everyday, at sunrise, they would approach their father and bow at his feet. One would say, 'My Lord, with your blessings, all joys are bestowed upon us.' The other would say, 'Your Majesty, one only gets the fruits of one's actions.'

"One day, the king got very angry with his second daughter and said to his ministers, 'Give this girl of mine away in marriage to any stranger you come across, so that she gets the fruits of her actions.'

—'It will be done, Your Majesty,' replied the ministers.

"Now, in their search for a stranger, the ministers came across this prince, who was living in the temple, and they married off the princess to him.

"The princess was very happy with the marriage and looked upon her husband as God. Shortly after their marriage, the prince and princess set out for another part of the country. On the way, the princess left her husband to rest under a tree and went into the nearby town to buy oil, salt, rice and other provisions. After making the necessary purchases, she returned to find the prince fast asleep.

"Suddenly, she saw a snake emerging from the prince's mouth and yet another from an ant-hill near by. Now both these snakes had come out for fresh air. When they saw each other, they got very annoyed. 'You wicked creature!' said the ant-hill snake to the other. 'Why are

you torturing this handsome prince? If he would only
drink a gruel, made of cummin seed and mustard, you
would surely be dead!'
—'Well,' replied the other, 'you, too, could be destroyed,
if someone poured hot water or hot oil on the ant-hill.
Then he could get the two pots of gold that you are
guarding.'

"The princess, who was standing behind a tree, heard
their argument and came to know their secrets. She
acted accordingly. As a result, her husband recovered
his health and, at the same time, they had two pots of
gold to themselves.

—"And so," continued Prakarakarna, "that's why I said,

'Those who refuse to co-operate,
Shall be destroyed like the two snakes.' "

When Arimaradana, the owl king, had heard
Prakarakarna's advice, he finally agreed that the crow
should not be killed.

Then Raktaksha said to the other ministers with a
smile, "Through your lack of understanding, some
disaster is bound to befall the master. I repeat once
again, the crow must be killed!"

But in spite of so much opposition from Raktaksha,
the owls did not listen and took the crow to their cave.

On the way, the crow suddenly cried out, "Oh, what
is the use of this miserable life? I shall end it by entering
the fire. Please don't stop me!"

—"Why do you intend entering fire?" asked Raktaksha.
—"Well," replied Sthirajeevi, "I have been reduced to
this plight by Meghavarana, because of you. Now, I
should like to be reborn an owl, so that I can have my
revenge on him."

Now, Raktaksha was an expert in the nitishastras and
so he said to the crow, "You speak very charmingly but
you are crooked! Even if you were reborn an owl, you
would still be a crow at heart. As the story goes:

'Turning down the offers of marriage
Made by the Sun God, the Cloud, the Lord of the

Wind, and the Mountain,
    A female mouse chose a husband of her own kind.' "
—"How was that?" asked the others.
And Raktaksha told:

THE STORY OF THE FEMALE MOUSE

"On the bank of the river Ganga*, there was a beautiful ashrama. The water from the river gushed down on rocks, making a tremendous noise, which frightened the fishes. It whirled round and round, and the water was a mass of foam.

"Now, in this ashrama lived Tapasvis, who were always absorbed in meditation. Their bodies had grown lean with fasting, penance and rigorous self-discipline. They ate roots and fruits and drank only holy water from the Ganga. They wore clothes made of bark.

"The Kulapati* of this ashrama was one Yadnyavalkya*. One day, while he was bathing in the holy water of the Ganga and offering his prayers, a mouse, dropped by a hawk, fell into his hands. Yadnyavalkya plucked a leaf from a nearby banyan tree and put the mouse on it. Then he took a second bath, to purify himself, because he had been contaminated by touching the mouse. By the power of meditation, he transformed the female mouse into a little girl. Then he took her home to the ashrama and said to his wife, 'My dear wife, we have no child of our own, so please take this little girl and bring her up carefully, as our own daughter.'

"And so, the child was brought up with great care until she attained the age of twelve. When Yadnyavalkya's wife noticed that the girl had reached the marriageable age, she said to her husband, 'My dear husband, the time for our daughter's marriage is slipping by. Please give it a serious thought.'

—'You are right,' he replied. 'I shall give her to someone who really deserves her. They say:

"Enter into marriage ties and friendship
Only with those who are, socially and financially,
Your equals."

And,

"A wise man should give his daughter in marriage

To someone who fulfils the following seven
    requirements:
Good family, good character, the capability to look
    after a family,
Education, wealth, physical fitness and suitable age."
—'And so, if the girl agrees, I shall summon Ravi* and
give her to him.'
—'Yes,' replied his wife, 'please do that.'
"By the power of invocation, Yadnyavalkya summoned
the Sun God to him. In a moment he appeared before
him and said, 'Maharishi*, why have you called me?'
—'Here is my daughter,' replied Yadnyavalkya. 'If she
is willing to marry you, please accept her hand.'
"Then he asked his daughter, 'Do you accept the Sun
God, who lights up the worlds?'
—'Father,' she replied, 'he is too fiery-tempered. I don't
want to marry him. Find me someone better!'
"So, the Rishi said to the Sun God, 'My Lord, is there
anyone better than you?'
—'Yes,' replied the Sun God. 'Megha* is superior to
me, for when he covers me, I am no longer visible.'
"And so the Rishi invited the Cloud and asked his
daughter, 'My child, may I offer your hand to the
Cloud?'
—'Father,' she replied, 'he is dark and too cold. I don't
want to marry him. Find me someone better!'
"So, the Rishi said to Megha, 'Oh Cloud, is there
anyone better than you?'
—'Yes,' replied the Cloud. 'Vayu* is superior to me, for
he makes me drift.'
"And so, the Rishi invited the Lord of the Wind and
said to his daughter, 'What do you say to him?'
—'Father,' she replied, 'he is very changeable. I don't
want to marry him. Find me someone better.'
"So, the Rishi said to the Lord of the Wind, 'My Lord,
is there anyone better than you?'
—'Yes,' replied the Lord of the Wind. 'The Mountain
is superior to me, for, although I am strong, he prevents

me from blowing where I want to.'

"And so, the Rishi invited the Mountain and said to his daughter, 'Now I am offering you to him.'

—'Father,' she replied, 'he is very hard and immovable. I don't want to marry him. Find me someone better.'

"So, the Rishi said to the Mountain, 'Oh Mountain! Is there anyone better than you?'.

—'Yes,' replied the Mountain. 'The mice are superior to me, for they bore holes in my body.'

"And so, the Rishi invited the king of mice and said to his daughter, 'Now, my little daughter, I'm going to offer you to this king of mice. Do you like him?'

"When the girl looked at the king of mice, her whole body began to quiver with delight and she said to her father, 'Oh father, he is the best of all! Please transform me into a mouse, so that after my marriage to the king of mice, I shall be able to perform the household duties of my new clan.'

"By the power of his meditation, the Rishi turned her back into a mouse and gave her in marriage to the king of mice.

—"And so," continued Raktaksha, "that's why I said,
    'Turning down the offers of marriage
    Made by the Sun God, the Cloud, the Lord of the
        Wind, and the Mountain,
    A female mouse chose a husband of her own kind.'

—"Therefore, even if this crow is reborn an owl, he would still be a crow at heart. So we must kill him."

However, in utter disregard of Raktaksha's advice, the owls took the crow right into their cave. On the way, the crow smiled in his heart of hearts and thought to himself, "Raktaksha alone is an expert in the knowledge of nitishastras, for he was right in advising them that I should be killed. If they had listened to him, there would have been no possibility of their coming to harm."

When they reached the entrance of the cave, Arimaradana, the owl king, said to his servants, "Please assign the crow a suitable place in the cave. This

Sthirajeevi is our well-wisher."

When Sthirajeevi heard this, he thought to himself, "I have to work out a plan to destroy these owls. Now, if I stay amongst them, they may get suspicious and discover from my behaviour, my real purpose. So I shall stay at the cave entrance and plan what I have in mind."

So, he said to the king of the owls, "Your Majesty, it's very nice of you, but I would prefer not to stay inside with you, for I belong to a clan which is your enemy. So, I'll stay here at the entrance of the cave. My Lord, I hold you in high esteem. The dust of your lotus feet shall sanctify me and I shall be your servant for ever."

—"Then, so be it," replied the king. And Sthirajeevi was given a comfortable place at the mouth of the cave.

By the order of Arimaradana, the servants began to feed Sthirajeevi on various choice foods and bits of flesh and, in a few days, he became as fit as a peacock.

When Raktaksha saw the crow being well fed and getting fat, he said to the king. "Your Majesty! I think all of you are being very unwise. As the bird said:

'First I was foolish, then the hunter,
Then the ministers and then the king,
We are all a pack of fools.' "

—"How was that?" asked the owls.

And Raktaksha told:

THE STORY OF THE HUNTER AND THE BIRD
WHOSE DROPPINGS TURNED TO GOLD

"On the top of a mountain, there was a huge tree. In the tree, lived a certain bird, by the name of Sindhuka*, whose droppings always turned to gold.

"One day, a hunter came to the spot to catch birds. While he was watching, this bird discharged its droppings and immediately it turned into a piece of gold. The hunter was wonder-struck and he thought to himself, 'I have been catching birds since I was a small child, but never have I seen the droppings of a bird turn to gold!'

"So the hunter set a trap in the tree. The foolish bird did not notice either the hunter or the trap and was caught. The hunter took him out of the trap and put him in a cage.

"Then he thought to himself, 'Now, before anyone finds out about this strange bird and reports it to the king, I had better go to him myself and show the bird.'

"And so, he took the bird to the king and told him everything. The king was delighted and said to his attendants, 'Look after this bird carefully. Give him food and water to his heart's content.'

"But the king's ministers said to him, 'Your Majesty! How can you trust the words of a mere hunter? Could it ever be possible to get gold from a bird's droppings? We advise you to take him out of the cage and release him.' The king listened to his ministers' advice and set the bird free. Immediately, he perched himself on top of a nearby gate and let fall his droppings which immediately turned to gold. And he said,

'First I was foolish, then the hunter,
　Then the ministers and then the king,
　We are all a pack of fools.' "

—"In the same way," continued Raktaksha, "we are all fools for sparing this crow. We must kill him!"

But still the owls turned a deaf ear to Raktaksha's advice and continued to lavish attention on the crow.

The Raktaksha called his followers together and said to them in confidence, "Until now, we have been safe here, but I have a foreboding of an approaching disaster. I have done my best to convince Arimaradana of my point of view, but in vain. So we must leave this place and go where we shall be safe. As the jackal said,

'He who anticipates the coming of a disaster,
And acts accordingly, is spared,
But he who fails to anticipate it,
Comes to grief:
I have grown old living in this jungle,
But I have never yet heard a cave talking!' "

—"How was that?" asked his friends.

And Raktaksha told:

THE STORY OF THE LION, THE JACKAL AND THE CAVE

"In a certain part of the jungle, there lived a lion, by the name of Kharanakhara*. One day, he felt hungry and wandered everywhere looking for food, but he could not catch a single animal.

"At sunset, he went into a big cave, thinking to himself, 'Some animal is bound to be living here and will certainly return during the evening. I shall hide in the cave and wait for him.'

"Sure enough, after a short time, a jackal, by the name of Dadhiputcha*, arrived on the scene. He noticed that a lion's footprints were leading into the cave but not coming out. He thought to himself, 'Now I am dead! It is almost certain that there is a lion inside. But how can I know for sure? What can I do to find out?'

"Suddenly an idea struck him. He stood at the entrance of the cave and began to shout, 'Hello, Cave! Cave!' He waited in silence for some time. Then he cried, 'Ho, Cave! Don't you remember the agreement we came to, that when I arrive here, I shall first call you and you will reply, and only then will I come in? Now, as you are not replying, I shall go to some other cave.'

"When the lion heard this, he thought to himself, 'The cave really replies to the jackal when he returns, but today, for fear of me, it is keeping quiet. As they say:

"When fear takes a hold on you,
You are paralysed,
Not a word will come out of your mouth."

—'So, I shall invite him in myself and when he enters, I'll make a meal of him.'

"With this idea in mind, the lion replied to the jackal, 'Hello, jackal! It's all right for you to come in.'

"The cave echoed with his roar so loud that even animals far away were frightened. The jackal too bolted, saying to himself,

'He who anticipates the coming of a disaster,
And acts accordingly, is spared,
But he who fails to anticipate it,
Comes to grief:
I have grown old living in this jungle,
But I have never yet heard a cave talking!'
—"Similarly," continued Raktaksha, "I too anticipate a disaster. Think over what I have said and leave with me."

Raktaksha's followers listened to his advice and flew off with him to a far away country.

Sthirajeevi was very pleased when he heard of Raktaksha's departure, thinking to himself, "His leaving is extremely beneficial to me, for he was far-sighted, but these here are stupid and I can easily destroy them, for they say:

'When the king's ministers lack foresight,
The king does not rule for long.' "

Pretending that he wanted to make a nest for himself, the crow began to bring small twigs and make a pile of them at the entrance of the cave. The foolish owls did not realise that the crow was doing all this to roast them alive later on. It's true what they say:

"An ill-fated man
Considers his enemies his friends
And destroys his real friends
He mistakes good for evil
And evil for good."

When the crow had piled up enough twigs at the entrance of the cave, he waited until noon (for the owls were blind during the day) and then flew off to Meghavarana, the king of the crows.

When he arrived at the king's court, he said to him, "My Lord, I have prepared the enemy's stronghold in such a way that it can easily be burnt. So, come with all your followers, every one of you, carrying pieces of burning wood in your beaks, and throw them at the entrance of the cave. Then all our enemies will be burnt to death!"

—"But," said the king, his face beaming with joy, "stop a minute. First tell me the news! It's so long since I saw you!"

—"This is not the proper time to talk," said Sthirajeevi, "for it's possible that some enemy spy may see me and report to the owl king. And if that happens, they will all escape, for they say:

'He who delays work,

That should be finished quickly,

Enrages the gods

Who put obstacles in his way.'

—"So, I shall tell you everything after we have completely wiped out the enemy and returned home."

After listening to Sthirajeevi's advice, Meghavarana and his followers, each took a piece of burning wood in their beaks and followed Sthirajeevi to the owl's cave. Then they threw their burning brands on to the pile of twigs, collected by Sthirajeevi, and soon a huge fire began to blaze. The owls now realised what was happening and remembered Raktaksha's advice, but as they were blind by day, they could not find their way out and they all perished in the flames.

And so, with their enemy completely wiped out, Meghavarana and the other crows returned to the old banyan tree. Their king seated himself on the throne and said happily to Sthirajeevi, "Now Tata, tell us how you spent your days amongst the enemy. I believe, living amongst the enemy is like sitting on the sharp edge of a sword."

—"I do agree with you," said Sthirajeevi, "but I had to put up with this ordeal, in order to destroy the owls. And, surprisingly enough, they had only one clever and intelligent minister amongst them, an owl by the name of Raktaksha. He guessed that something of the kind was in my mind and escaped with a few of his followers. The others were complete fools and had no understanding of diplomacy. They did not even know that:

'Someone who has left the service of the enemy,
And come over to the other side,
Should never be trusted;
He should always be avoided.'
—"Yes, Your Majesty, it's true that living amongst the
enemy is like sitting on the sharp edge of a sword. I
know from experience. But then they say:
'A fellow who is cunning,
Puts up with his enemy
Even under demanding conditions,
Unperturbed, both by honour and insult,
He bides his time,
In order, ultimately, to achieve his objective.
Thus, a black snake allowed frogs to ride on his
back
And eventually he ate them all up.' "
—"How was that?" asked Meghavarana.
And Sthirajeevi told:

THE STORY OF THE FROGS AND
THE BLACK SNAKE

"Near Varuna* mountain, there lived an old snake, by the name of Mandavishya*. One day, he thought to himself, 'I am getting too old to hunt for food. How could I manage to maintain myself without having to work hard for it?' Then he hit upon a plan. He went to a pond that was full of frogs and began to behave as though he was a Tapasvi, who had renounced the world. A frog came out of the water and asked him, 'Why aren't you moving about in search of food as usual?'

—'Ah,' replied the snake, 'unfortunate fellow that I am! I no longer have any desire for food. I'll explain to you. Last night, when I was wandering about in search of food, I saw a frog. When I tried to catch him, he got frightened and jumped in amongst a group of Brahmins, who were reciting the Vedas, and vanished. I could not reach him there, so I sat waiting for him to come out. Meanwhile my eyes fell on a Brahmin's son and I bit him. He died on the spot. His father was heart-broken and he cursed me with these words:
—"Wicked demon of a serpent! You have bitten my son and killed him when he did nothing to you. For this, from today on, you shall serve the frogs and they will use you to ride on. You will live off whatever they are pleased to offer you." '
—'And so,' said the snake, 'I have come to serve you!'

"When the frog heard the snake's story, he went and told it to the others. Finally, the king of frogs came to know the story. He thought it very strange and visited the snake himself in the company of his ministers, in order to ascertain the facts. After the snake had assured him that his life would be safe, the king climbed on his back. Other frogs also took their turns, according to age. And those who did not find any place on the snake's back, hopped after him. To please the frogs, the snake exhibited to them various types of crawling.

"The king of the frogs was delighted and he said, 'I have never had so much pleasure riding an elephant, a horse, a carriage or a human being, as by riding this snake!'

"Next day, the snake started crawling slowly on purpose. When the king noticed this, he asked him, 'Friend, why aren't you crawling as you usually do?' —'I've had nothing to eat!' replied the snake. 'I'm too weak to crawl properly.' So the frog king replied, 'All right then, you can eat small frogs.'

"When the snake heard this, he pretended to be surprised and said, 'Well, well! This is exactly the second part of the Brahmin's curse come true, for he said that I should have to live on whatever the frogs were pleased to offer me. Your Majesty, your kindness makes me very happy.'

"After that, the snake began to eat small frogs daily and, in a short time, he became very strong.

"The snake thought to himself with a smile, 'I have beguiled them enough to allow me to eat the small frogs, but how long will this supply last?'

"Jalapada*, the frog king, was so completely taken in by the snake's talk that he did not understand his real motive.

"After a few days, a big black snake came to the same place. He was flabbergasted to see the frogs riding on Mandavishya and he said to him, 'Mandavishya, these frogs are our food! Why are you carrying them on your back? It is beneath you!' —'I do agree with you,' said Mandavishya, 'but I am playing it cool and waiting patiently.'

And he explained to him everything.

"One day, Mandavishya said with a laugh, 'Eating all these frogs, I have discovered different tastes.'

"And Jalapada, the frog king, hearing this, was dumb-founded and said to the snake, 'My good fellow, what kind of talk is that!'

"To cover up his slip, the snake replied, 'Oh, nothing at all.' And then, with his clever talk, he succeeded in putting the frog king at ease.

"In due course, the snake started eating even the larger frogs and in the end, he ate the frog king himself and all the frogs were utterly wiped out.

—"And so," continued Sthirajeevi, that's why I said,

'A fellow who is cunning,
Puts up with his enemy
Even under demanding conditions,
Unperturbed, both by honour and insult,
He bides his time,
In order, ultimately, to achieve his objective.
Thus, a black snake allowed frogs to ride on his
    back
And eventually he ate them all up.'

—"Your Majesty, just as through cunning, Mandavishya ate up the entire population of the frogs, in the same way, I annihilated the owls. As they say:

'A forest fire burns down the trees
But the roots lie safe underneath;
Whilst a cold frosty wind
Destroys the very roots.' "

—"Yes, indeed Tata," replied the king. "But it pleases me most that you have completely uprooted our enemies, the owls. As they say:

A small amount of debt unpaid,
The last trace of fire left unextinguished,
The last trace of sickness uncured after treatment,
And enemies surviving a battle,
All these will rise again and again
Unless they are utterly destroyed.'

—"You have indeed proved your worth, for they say:

'Inferior people never begin a task for fear of
    destruction,
Ordinary people give up a task only half-finished
    because of obstruction,

But superior people will never give up anything,
However many difficulties may beset them.' "

—"You are right, in what you say," said Sthirajeevi,
"but, to do it, you need not only bravery but skill as
well. The clever man achieves his ends with maximum
attention to detail. As they say:

'Those who look down on insignificant work,
Because they think it's too easy,
Do it carelessly,
And, one day, regret it.'

—"But, Your Majesty! Now that all our enemies have
been destroyed, I would advise you to devote your
attention solely to the welfare of your subjects, for:

'A king who does not protect his subjects,
Is as useless as an old goat's hanging neck teat;
But, a king who loves virtue, and hates vices
And appreciates good servants,
Will enjoy his kingdom for ages.'

And,

'A king should not be deceived by the magnificence
of kingship
For although it is as difficult to acquire
As to climb up a bamboo,
Yet it may vanish in a moment.
It is as fidgety as a monkey,
As detached as drops of dew on a Lotus leaf,
As changeable as the wind,
As unreliable as the friendship of the wicked,
As transient as the colours in the sky at sunset,
And as unstable as water bubbles.'

—"And so, Your Majesty," continued Sthirajeevi, "know
this and rule justly over your kingdom. Then you will
find happiness."

THE END OF
THE THIRD TANTRA

THE FORFEIT OF PROFITS

This is the beginning of the fourth tantra called, "The forfeit of profits" and here is the first verse:

"A man who does not lose his head,
In the face of calamities,
Shall overcome them,
Just like the monkey in the midst of the sea."

The story goes like this:

On a sea beach, there stood a big Jambu* tree, which bore fruit throughout the year. In the tree, there lived a monkey, by the name of Raktamukha*.

One day, a crocodile called Karalamukha*, who lived in a creek, came out and made himself comfortable on the soft sand under the tree.

At this, the monkey spoke to him with these words, "You are my guest. Please accept this sweet nectareous fruit of the Jambu tree, for:

'All the gods, and his ancestors too,
Will turn away their faces,
From the man who lets a guest leave his house
Sighing and unhonoured.' "

With these words, the monkey gave him the Jambu fruit. When he had devoured it, the crocodile chatted with the monkey for a long time and finally went home.

In this way, sitting under the shade of the Jambu tree, the crocodile and the monkey used to spend their time together, devouring the Jambu fruit and talking pleasantly about various moral tales and so on. After the crocodile had had his fill, he would take home what was left over, for his wife.

One day, his wife said to him, "Darling! Where do you get such sweet nectareous fruit everyday?"

—"Dearest," replied the crocodile, "I have a bosom friend, a monkey, by the name of Raktamukha, who is very affectionate towards me and gives me this fruit."

At this, his wife said, "Someone who eats this nectareous fruit everyday, must also have a heart as sweet as nectar. Now, if you really love me, bring home his heart so that I can eat it, thereby escape old age and death, and enjoy life with you."

The crocodile replied, "Darling! Please, please, don't talk like that! I now regard him as my brother and besides, he is very kind to me and gives me the fruit. So, how can I kill him? Give up your demand, for they say:

'Brotherhood developed by way of conversation,
  Is reputed to be far superior
  To brotherhood that comes from having the same
      mother.' "

-"So far," said the crocodile's wife, "you have never turned down any of my requests. So, I think this must be some female monkey whom you love and spend the whole day with. Now I understand you very well. You don't even speak nicely to me any more and give me what I ask for. At night time, when we are together, your sighs are as hot as a flame of fire, but not for me! You don't hug and kiss me as passionately as you used to either. Hypocrite! I believe some other sweet thing lives in your heart nowadays."

The crocodile fell down at her feet in great distress. Then he got up and took her on his lap and, speaking lovingly to her, said, "Dearest! Why are you getting angry with me, when I fall at your feet like a slave?"

When she heard him say this, the crocodile's wife replied, with tears in her eyes, "Deceiver! With all your amorous gestures, you are trying to fool me, but some other female lives in your heart. Why make fun of me by falling at my feet! And anyway, if she is not your beloved, why can't you kill her, when I tell you to? If, on the other hand, it's a male monkey, how could there be love between you and him? What more is there for me to say. If I don't have that heart, then know for certain that I shall starve myself to death."

When he heard her resolution, the crocodile was very worried and he said to himself, "Ah, how true it is what they say:

'Glue, an idiot, a woman, a crab,
A shark, indigo dye and a drunkard,
Once they attach themselves to something
They will never let go.'

—"So, what shall I do! How shall I kill the monkey?"

With these thoughts, the crocodile went to see his friend.

When the monkey saw the crocodile arriving, looking very glum, he asked him, "Friend! Why are you late today? You don't look at all cheerful and you aren't reciting any verses as you usually do."

—"Well," replied the crocodile, "your sister* gave me a vicious telling off today. She said, 'Ungrateful fellow! Don't you show me your face again! Everyday you take advantage of this friend of yours, but not once have you brought him home and entertained him here! Now, unless you do so, I will see you in the next life!' Well, time elapsed while I was arguing with her and I was delayed. So now, please come home with me. Your sister has set up a bower in your honour and decorated the entrance of the house with the trunks of the plantain trees and mango leaves. She has dressed herself in beautiful clothes and put on ornaments and jewels, and now she is waiting anxiously at the gate to receive you."

—"My friend," said the monkey, "my sister has spoken well, for they say:

'There are six indications of friendship:
Giving and receiving,
Listening to and telling secrets,
Entertaining and being entertained.'

—"But I am a jungle dweller and you live in water. So, how could I possibly come to your home? It would be better if you brought my sister over here, so that I can bow to her and receive her blessings."

—"But, friend," replied the crocodile, "it is better if you

come to us! My house is on a very charming sandy
bank, just across the creek, but you can ride on my
back across the water. Come on, don't be afraid!"
—"My friend!" said the monkey delightedly. "If that's
the case, what are we waiting for? Hurry up! Look, I
am already on your back!" And so, with the monkey
riding on his back, the crocodile entered the sea.

When the crocodile started swimming fast in deep
water, the monkey got frightened and he said, "Brother!
Please go very slowly. My body is getting drenched by
the waves of the sea!"

Then the crocodile thought to himself, "He is entirely
in my power in this deep water. He can't even move.
So, I will tell him my real purpose in bringing him here
and then he can pray to his chosen deity."

So, he said to the monkey, "My dear fellow, I have
brought you here to kill you, at the express request of
my wife. So, you had better pray to your chosen deity!"
—"Brother!" exclaimed the monkey. "What wrong have
I ever done you or your wife that you should think of
killing me?"
—"She wants to eat your heart," said the crocodile. "She
thinks it must be as sweet as nectar, because you eat
nectareous fruit everyday. She says, it will save her from
old age and death. That is why I have played this trick
on you."
—"Friend," said the ready-witted monkey, "if that's the
case, whyever didn't you tell me earlier, over at my
place? You see, I always keep my heart in the hollow
of the Jambu tree for safety. I would gladly have handed
it over to you for my sister. If you are taking me to
your home without my heart, the whole thing will be
pointless!"
—"Well then," said the crocodile, "I will take you back
to the Jambu tree to get it." So, the crocodile took the
monkey back to the beach. On the way, the monkey
kept murmuring prayers to the gods.

As soon as they reached the shore, the monkey sprang

up the Jambu tree and thought to himself, "Phew! I've
got back my life! It's true what they say:
> 'Never trust a man who is not to be trusted,
> Or even a trustworthy man beyond reasonable limits,
> For it is dangerous to do so
> And can result in utter ruin.'

—"Oh, today is like regeneration to me!"

While he was thinking this, the crocodile said to him,
"Ho! Friend! Hand me over your heart then, so that I
can take it to my wife. She can eat it and give up her
fast."

The monkey laughed loudly and ridiculed the
crocodile, "Treacherous fool! How could anybody leave
his heart behind? Get away from here and never come
back again! It's true what they say:

> 'A man who wants to be friends with someone
> Who has let him down before
> Surely courts his own death.' "

When the crocodile heard this, he was very embarrassed
and started thinking, "What a fool I was to give away
my secret! Now, if it is possible, I must try to re-establish
his confidence in me."

So he said, "My dear friend! I was only joking, to test
you. What would your sister want with your heart? Now,
come on, be my guest. My wife must be anxiously waiting
to meet you."

—"Wicked devil!" said the monkey. "After this, I shall
never come again. As the king of the frogs said:

> 'What sin will a starving man not commit?
> Weak people become cruel,
> Madam! Please tell Priyadarshana*
> That Gangadatta* will never again return to the
>   well.' "

—"How was that?" asked the crocodile.
And the monkey told:

THE STORY OF THE KING OF FROGS AND
THE SNAKE

"In a certain well there lived a king of frogs, by the name of Gangadatta.

"He was tormented by the nagging of his relatives, so he climbed up the water-wheel and slipped out, thinking to himself, 'How can I have revenge on them, for they say:

"When you are in trouble and someone does you
    harm,
Or when you are in difficulties and someone jeers
    at you,
By paying them back in their own coin,
I believe, you are regenerated." '

"While he was thinking this, the frog king saw a snake going into his hole. He thought to himself, 'I know what I will do. I will take this snake down into the well and get all my relatives eaten up. It's true what they say:

"A wise man should uproot his strong enemies
By pitting them against each other
And getting them to destroy each other.
A thorn is taken out by another thorn
And then, they are both thrown away.
Thus pain is turned into joy." '

"Thinking this over, the frog king went and stood outside the entrance of the snake's hole and called, 'Ho, you! Priyadarshana! Come out!'

"When the snake heard this, he thought to himself, 'I am sure that is not one of my own kith and kin calling me, for he speaks differently from us. And anyway, I have no friends whatsoever. So, I'll stay right inside my hole until I find out who he is, for Brihaspati has said:

"A man should never be friendly with someone
Whose family, character, temperament

And place of residence,
He does not know."
—'Perhaps the person who is calling me, wants to
   catch me, using the enticement of Mantra*, flute
   music or herbs.'
"So cautiously he called out, 'Who is it?'
"The frog king replied, 'I am Gangadatta, the king of
frogs, and I have come to make friends with you.'
—'Well!' said the snake. 'That is very hard to believe!
Can grass and fire ever be friends? They say:
"Even in dreams,
Never approach anyone
Who could cause your death."
—'So why are you talking such nonsense!'
—'What you say is true,' said Gangadatta. 'You are
indeed my natural enemy. But I am being tormented
to death and I have come to you for your help. I want
you to eat my enemies.'
—'Tell me,' said the snake, 'who is tormenting you?'
—'It's my relatives!' said Gangadatta.
—'Well,' said the snake, 'where do you live? In a well,
a pond, or a lake?'
—'In a well, built of layers of stone!' replied Gangadatta.
—'But I have no legs,' said the snake, 'how can I get
into the well? And even if I could, where could I sit
and eat your relatives? Go away!'
—'Please!' said Gangadatta. 'I will show you how to get
into the well comfortably and inside, at the edge of the
water level, there is a very nice hole where you can sit
and eat them. Come with me.'
"When he heard this, the snake thought to himself,
'I have grown old and can't even catch a mouse without
great difficulty. Now this fellow, an enemy of his own
species, is showing me a way to live in comfort. I shall
go and live there. It's true what they say:
"A wise man, whose limbs have grown weak
And has no source of income,
Should always arrange things in such a way

That he continues to earn his livelihood without
    any effort." '

"And so, the snake said aloud, 'Gangadatta, if this is
rea..y true, then lead the way and I shall follow you.'

"Gangadatta replied, 'I shall take you by an easy route
and show you the hiding place, but you must spare my
own friends. Eat only the ones I point out to you.'

—'We are friends now,' said the snake, 'so don't be
afraid. I shall do exactly as you've told me.'

"With these words, the snake came out, embraced the
frog king and started along with him. When they reached
the well, the frog king led the snake down by way of
the water-wheel and took him to the hole. He made
the snake comfortable and then pointed out to him
those relatives who were not on good terms with him.
And, one by one, the snake ate them up.

"When these frogs had been exhausted, the snake said
to the frog king, 'Please, give me some food! After all,
it was you who brought me here, so you are responsible
to feed me.'

—'Snake,' said the frog king, 'you have done me a
friendly service. Now go home the way you came down
the water-wheel.'

—'Gangadatta!' said the snake. 'That's not fair! The hole
where I used to live, must have been occupied by
someone else by now. No, I will stay here. Go on giving
me your relatives one by one. If you don't, I will eat
up every one of you!'

"When the frog king heard this, he was overwhelmed
with grief and he thought to himself, 'What a stupid
thing I have done in bringing the snake here. If I
oppose him, he will eat us all. It's true what they say:

"There is no doubt about it:
    Making friends with a stronger enemy
    Amounts to eating a poisonous pill."

—'So everyday, I will allow him to eat a friend, for they
say:

"Seeing the enemy ready to grab everything,

A wise man placates him by offering him a little
And thus, for a time, keeps him at bay,
Just as the ocean placates the subaqueous fire
By offering it a small quantity of water,
From time to time."

And,

"When a complete loss is imminent,
A wise man gives half away voluntarily
And works with the rest,
For a complete loss is unbearable."

And again,

"A wise man never sacrifices big interests
For smaller ones."

—'This is real wisdom!'

"So, the frog king came to a decision and he began
to offer the snake one frog everyday. The snake ate
what was offered to him and also began to eat the other
frogs as well, without the knowledge of the frog king.

"One day, the snake also ate up Jamnadatta*, the son
of Gangadatta, along with some others.

"When Gangadatta came to know this, he began to
wail in a loud voice, 'Oh, the wretched fellow that I
am!' And he was inconsolable.

"Then his wife said to him, 'What is the good of
crying now? You are the cause of the destruction of
your own kith and kin. Who will rescue us? You had
better work out a plan to escape or else to kill the
snake.'

"Now, in due course, all the frogs were finished off.
Only Gangadatta was left. Then Priyadarshana said to
the frog king, 'Gangadatta, I am hungry! There are no
frogs left. Please get me something to eat, for after all,
you brought me here.'

—'My friend,' replied Gangadatta, 'as long as I am here,
you have no need to worry on any account. Now, if
you allow me to leave this well and go to another one,
I shall win the confidence of other frogs and bring
them here.'

—'You have been like a brother to me!' said the snake. 'I shall never eat you. Now, if you carry out what you have promised, you will be to me like a father. So, please go.'

"And so, Gangadatta offered prayers to innumerable gods and left the well.

"The snake waited anxiously for his return, but all in vain. After a long time Priyadarshana said to a female lizard living near by, 'Madam, please give me a little help. You have known Gangadatta for a long time. Would you find him for me in one of the other wells and give him a message? Tell him, "If the other frogs aren't coming, at least you return quickly. I can't bear to be separated from you." And tell him, "If I harm you, may I lose all the merits I have earned in my life so far!" '

"The lizard found Gangadatta in one of the other wells and said, 'Gangadatta! Your friend Priyadarshana is anxiously waiting for your return. He won't harm you. He has staked all his good deeds as a guarantee for your safety. So come along, don't be afraid.'

—'But,' Gangadatta replied, 'what sin will a starving man not commit? Weak people become cruel. Madam! Please tell Priyadarshana that Gangadatta will never again return to the well.'

"And with those words, he sent her away.

—"And so, wicked water-dweller," continued the monkey, "like Gangadatta, I too shall never go to your home again."

When the crocodile heard this, he said, "My friend! It is not proper for you to behave like this. Please come so that I can free myself from the sin of ingratitude, or else I shall begin a fast and starve myself to death at the foot of this very tree."

—"You fool!" replied the monkey. "Do you think that I am as stupid as Lambakarana* who, even when he sensed danger, still allowed himself to be killed? They say:

'He came, then ran away,
When he saw the prowess of the lion,
But fool that he was, without heart or ears,
He came back once again and was killed.' "
—"How was that?" asked the crocodile.
And the monkey told:

THE STORY OF THE LION AND THE DONKEY

"In a certain jungle, there lived a lion, by the name of Karalakesara*. He had a servant, a jackal named Dhusaraka*, who was his constant companion.

"Now, once the lion fought a very fierce battle with an elephant and his body was so severely wounded that he was unable to walk. Consequently, Dhusaraka too began to starve and became very weak.

"One day, he said to the lion, 'Master! I am starving and I can't even walk a single step. How then can I serve you!'

—'Well, my friend,' said the lion, 'go and search for an animal that I can kill even in my present condition.'

"So, the jackal started on a search and arrived at a nearby village. There he noticed a lean donkey, by the name of Lambakarana, eating grass along the bank of the river with great difficulty.

"The jackal approached the donkey and said, 'Uncle! Greetings! I am seeing you after a long time. Tell me, why have you become so thin?'

—'Nephew!' he replied. 'What can I tell you? The cruel washerman, my master, tortures me with heavy burdens and never gives me so much as a handful of clean grass. So I have to eat this grass, mixed with dust. How then would my body be fat?'

—'Uncle!' replied the jackal. 'If that's the case, then I know a very pleasant place where the grass is as green as emerald. Come along with me and you can stay there. We will pass our days happily, telling each other moral stories and talking about philosophy.'

—'Nephew!' said the donkey. 'How nice of you to say so! But we villagers are easily killed by jungle animals, so what good would such a spot be to me?'

—'Uncle,' said the jackal, 'please don't talk like that. That part of the country is well protected by my powerful claws. No other animal dare enter there! For the very same reason, because they were being tortured by their masters, three she-donkeys are living there too. They are young and well fed. They said to me, "If you are really our uncle, please find us some suitable husband in one of the villages." That's why I am taking you there.'

"When the donkey heard the jackal's words, he was fired with lust and said, 'Well, if that's the case, you go ahead and I'll follow you. It's true what they say:

"If desire arises in a man's heart,
Merely by hearing a woman mentioned,
It would indeed be astonishing,
If he did not feel passionate
When he actually saw her." '

"And so, enticed in this way, the donkey went with the jackal to the lion. As soon as the suffering lion saw the donkey, he got up and tried to strike him with his paw, but missed. And the donkey ran for his life.

"When the donkey had gone, the jackal said angrily to the lion, 'Is that the way you aim a blow! Even a donkey can escape from you. So, how could you fight an elephant?'

"The lion smiled shamefacedly and said, 'What could I do? I wasn't ready to attack him, otherwise even an elephant would not escape me.'

—'Well,' said the jackal, 'I will bring him to your presence once more, but this time stay on the alert to attack him.'

—'My dear fellow,' said the lion, 'how will he come back, when he actually saw me and ran away? Please find some other animal.'

—'What's that to do with you?' said the jackal. 'All you have to do is to stay ready to attack.'

"Then the jackal followed the donkey's trail and saw him grazing in the same place.

"When the donkey saw the jackal, he cried, 'Nephew! You took me to a really nice place! I nearly fell into the jaws of death! Tell me, who was that animal whose lightning blows I so narrowly escaped?'

"Then the jackal said with a smile, 'Uncle! It was a female donkey, who wanted to embrace you when she saw you. But you, like a coward, ran away. So, come on now. She has said that she will starve herself to death because of you. "If Lambakarana does not become my husband," she told me, "I shall burn myself in fire or drown myself in water. I cannot bear to be separated from him." So please come to her or you will be responsible for the death of a female and Kamadeva will be angry with you. For they say:

"Fools, who, for the sake of useless
And imaginary ideas of heavenly comforts,
Give up charming women,
Who would bring them all happiness,
Arouse the anger of Kamadeva.
They turn into ascetics:
Get their heads shaved clean,
Walk about naked, wear saffron robes,
Grow their hair long
And carry skulls in their hands." '

"The donkey was once again coaxed into going with the jackal. This time, the lion was lying in wait for him and the donkey was killed.

"Afterwards, the lion asked the jackal to guard the donkey and went to the river to take a bath. The jackal could not control his hunger and ate up the donkey's heart and ears.

"When the lion returned from taking his bath and worshipping the gods and his forefathers, he found that the donkey's heart and the ears were missing. He turned on the jackal angrily and said, 'You villain! What have you done? You have polluted my food by eating his heart and ears.'

—'Please, master,' said the jackal, 'don't speak to me like that. This donkey had no heart or ears. Otherwise how would he have come back after once seeing you?'

"The lion believed him. He had his fill of the donkey and left the rest to the jackal.

—"And so," continued the monkey, "that's why I said:
   'He came, then ran away,
   When he saw the prowess of the lion,
   But fool that he was, without heart or ears,
   He came back once again and was killed.'
—"And you too are a fool," the monkey went on. "You
were out to deceive me but you spoiled the whole affair
by talking. It's true what they say:
   'A hypocrite with little intelligence,
   Who, forgetting his own interests,
   Speaks the truth,
   Will never succeed in achieving his objectives,
   Just like Yudhisthira*, the potter.' "
—"How was that?" asked the crocodile.
And the monkey told:

THE STORY OF THE POTTER CALLED YUDHISTHIRA

"In a certain town, there lived a potter, by the name of Yudhisthira. One day he was drunk, and, stumbling on the broken pots, fell down. The sharp edges caused a wound in his head and blood began to ooze out. With great difficulty, he got up. Owing to improper care, the wound got worse and even when, in the end, it was cured, it left a big scar on his forehead.

"After some time, there was famine in the country and the potter became very thin. Accompanied by some servants of the royal family, he went off to another part of the country, where he got himself employed in the king's service.

"When the king noticed the big scar on the potter's forehead, he thought, 'No doubt this wound on his forehead was caused when he was fighting face to face with an enemy. He is a very brave man.'

"So, the potter was placed amongst the princes with great honour. When they saw that he was being favoured by the king, undeservedly, they became jealous but could not say anything because they feared the king.

"One day, a battle was impending. The king invited all the warriors so that he could bestow honour on them and thus encourage them. While the elephants and the horses were being equipped and the soldiers inspected, the king took this potter aside and said, 'Prince! What is your name? What is your caste? And in which battle did you get this wound on your forehead?'

—'Your Majesty!' replied the potter. 'This wound wasn't caused by a sword! I am a potter by profession. And in my house there used to be many pots lying around. One day, I got drunk and tripped over some broken ones and that's what caused this scar on my forehead.'

"When the king heard this, he was very embarrassed and said to his soldiers, 'This potter has deceived me by pretending to be a prince. Drive him away quickly.'

"When they began to drive the potter away from the palace, he cried out, 'Stop! Please don't do that. Put me to the test in a battle.'

"The king replied, 'No doubt you have some excellent qualities but you would do better to go home for, as the lioness said to the young jackal:

"My son, it's true you are brave,
Good looking, intelligent and well educated,
But no elephants are killed in the family
You were born in." '

—'How was that?' asked the potter.
And the king told:

THE STORY OF THE LIONESS AND THE YOUNG JACKAL

" 'In a certain jungle, there lived a couple, a lion and lioness. One day, the lioness gave birth to two male cubs.

" 'Now, the lion would go out hunting and when he had killed the prey, he would bring it home and present it to the lioness.

" 'However, one day, he wandered everywhere in search of food but all in vain. Meanwhile, the sun set.

" 'As he was returning home, the lion came across a baby jackal. He did not kill him because he was only a baby. Catching hold of him carefully in his teeth, he took him home and presented him to his wife.

—"My dear," said the lioness, "have you brought some food?"

—"Dearest," replied the lion, "I was unable to catch anything today except this jackal. I thought to myself, 'It's only a baby, and belonging to our caste too, so I did not kill him, for they say:

"Never attack an ascetic, a Brahmin, a child or a woman

Or, in particular, someone who trusts you."

—"So, I have brought him home alive. However, you can eat him and manage for today. Tomorrow I shall secure some other prey."

—"My dear husband," said the lioness, "you wouldn't kill this baby, so how could I kill him and feed myself? As they say:

'Even when one's life is in danger,

It is not proper to forget one's obligations

And so commit a sin.'

—"This is our ancient religion. And so, I won't kill him but I shall look after him as my third son."

" 'So, she began to feed the baby jackal on her own milk and soon he became fat. The three babies began to grow up together without realising any difference between them and spent their childhood playing the same games.

" 'One day, a wild elephant appeared on the scene. When they saw him, the two lion cubs rushed forward furiously to attack him but the young jackal said, "Stop! He is an enemy of our species. Don't go near him!" And with these words, he ran home.

" 'The lion cubs also got discouraged because of their brother's cowardice. For they say:

"An energetic and plucky Commander,
Creates confidence in the whole army
But if he runs away,
Then the whole army falls into disarray."

" 'When the two cubs returned home, they told their parents, laughing, about their elder brother's behaviour. "When this fellow saw the elephant coming, he took to his heels."

" 'When the young jackal heard this, he got very excited. His lips quivered, his eyes grew red, furrows appeared on his forehead and he began to reprove the two cubs harshly.

" 'The lioness took him aside and said to him, "My dear, don't talk like that. After all they are your younger brothers."

" 'But the young jackal became still more angry and he said to her, "Am I in any way inferior to them in bravery, looks, education or intelligence, that they should ridicule me? I shall certainly kill them!"

" 'When the lioness heard this, she smiled within herself and, to save his life, she said to the young jackal, "My son, it's true you are brave, good looking, intelligent and well-educated, but no elephants are killed in the family you were born in. My child, listen. You are actually the son of a jackal, but I took pity on you and brought you up, giving you my milk. Now, before the cubs recognize you to be a jackal, go away from here and return to your own clan or they will kill you."

" 'When he heard this, the young jackal became frightened, fled from the place and joined his own clan. —'And so,' continued the king, 'that's why I say, that you would do better to run away from here, because if these warriors recognize you to be a potter, they would ridicule you and kill you.'

"When the potter heard this, he immediately left the palace.

—"And so," continued the monkey, "that's why I said:
'A hypocrite with little intelligence,
Who, forgetting his own interests,
Speaks the truth,
Will never succeed in achieving his objectives,
Just like Yudhisthira, the potter.'

—"You fool! You undertook to do this for the sake of your wife. A man should not be a slave to his wife. As Vararuchi* said:
'In what way doesn't a man
Do what a woman asks him to do?
On her request,
He neighs like a horse
And shaves his head at odd times.' "

—"How was that?" asked the crocodile.
And the monkey told:

THE STORY OF NANDA AND VARARUCHI

"Once upon a time, there lived a king, by the name of Nanda*. He ruled the entire land surrounded by the seas and his power was known far off, like the bright moon of autumn. The light reflecting from the crowns of many kings, who knelt before him, used to make the footstool, where he rested his feet, seem brightly coloured.

"The king had a minister called Vararuchi, an expert in politics and philosophy.

"One day, Vararuchi's wife was sulking. He adopted every tactics he could think of to bring her round, but failed. As a last resort, he said, 'My darling, I will do anything to make you happy.'

—'All right then!' she replied. 'Get your head shaved off and fall at my feet! Then I shall be happy.'

"The minister did so and his wife made up with him.

"In the same way, King Nanda's queen had a sulking fit. Her husband, the king, did his best to bring her round, but failed. Finally, he said to her, 'My darling, I will do anything to make you happy. Just say the word.'

—'All right then!' replied the queen. 'Let me put a bit in your mouth, ride you like a horse and make you gallop. And while you are running, you must neigh. If you do this, I will be happy.'

"The king did so and the queen became her usual self again.

"Early the following morning, when the king entered the court, he saw Vararuchi with his head shaved off. He said to him, 'Vararuchi! Why have you shaved your head all of a sudden?'

—'Your Majesty,' he replied, 'in what way doesn't a man do what a woman asks him to do? On her request, he neighs like a horse and shaves his head at odd times.'

—"And so," continued the monkey, "like Nanda and

Vararuchi, you too, wicked crocodile, are a slave to your
wife. You had conspired to kill me, but your chatter
gave you away. It's so true what they say:
>'Silence is golden,
>Parrots and other cackling birds get caught
>Whilst the cranes stay free.
>So, by keeping quiet one succeeds.'

And,
>'The donkey, who was dressed up in a tiger's skin,
>Was frightening to look at,
>But he got killed because he brayed.' "

—"How was that?" asked the crocodile.
And the monkey told:

THE STORY OF THE DONKEY AND
THE WASHERMAN

"In a town, there lived a washerman, by the name of Shuddhapata*. He had only one donkey. Because of lack of grass and other things to eat, the donkey had become very lean.

"One day, while the washerman was wandering in the jungle, he came across a dead tiger. He thought to himself, 'Oh, this is a piece of good luck. I know what I'll do. I'll put this tiger's skin on my donkey and let him loose in the barley fields at night time. The farmers will think it's a tiger and for fear of him, they won't come out.'

"This, the washerman did. From that time onward, the donkey would eat the barley to his heart's content during the night time, and early in the morning, the washerman would lead him back to the stall. With the passage of time, the donkey grew so fat that the washerman had to strain himself to drag the donkey back into the stall.

"One night, whilst the donkey was feeding in the barley fields, he heard a female donkey braying in the distance. He couldn't help braying in return. Immediately the farmers realised that it was only a donkey dressed up in a tiger's skin. They rushed out, caught hold of him and killed him with sticks.

—"And so," continued the monkey, "that's why I said,
    'The donkey, who was dressed up in a tiger's skin,
    Was frightening to look at,
    But he got killed because he brayed.' "

Now, while the crocodile and the monkey were talking, a water-dweller approached them and said to the crocodile, "Your wife was deprived of your love and has starved herself to death."

When the crocodile heard this, he was dumbfounded, as if struck by a thunderbolt. Heart-broken, he said to

the monkey, "Oh, what a calamity has befallen me! What
an unfortunate fellow I am, for they say:
    'He who has neither mother,
    Nor a sweet speaking wife in the house,
    Should go to the jungle,
    For to him, jungle and home are alike.'
—"My friend," continued the crocodile, "forgive me for
I have been treacherous towards you and now, as I
have lost my wife, I shall go into the fire and burn
myself."
  When the monkey heard this, he smiled and said,
"Foolish crocodile! Right from the beginning, I realised
that you were a slave to your wife and a hen-pecked
husband. And now I have proof. How stupid you are!
You grieve when you should be rejoicing. The death
of someone like that should be celebrated, for they say:
    'A wife of bad character,
    Who takes delight in always quarrelling,
    Brings her husband premature old age;
    So a man who seeks his own happiness,
    Should not even mention the name
    Of such a wicked woman.
    Women are very peculiar,
    They never say what they have on their minds
    Or on the tips of their tongues
    And what they do is always contrary to what they
      say.
    Those who are drawn to women by their enchanting
      appearances,
    Are destroyed, like moths in a flame.' "
  At this the crocodile said, "Friend, what you say is
quite true. But what shall I do now? Two calamities
have befallen me. First, the loss of my wife and second,
the loss of your friendship. This is what happens when
fate is hostile. As the female jackal said to the woman:
    'Naked woman!
    You are twice as clever as I am
    But you have now neither your lover nor your

    husband,
      So what are you staring at?' "
—"How was that?" asked the monkey.
And the crocodile told:

THE STORY OF THE FARMER'S WIFE

"In a certain town, there lived a farmer and his wife. As her husband was old, the woman was always thinking of other men and could never relax at home. The whole day she would wander about the town, looking for company.

"Once, a certain crook, who made it his business to rob other people, noticed her. When there was nobody else about, he went up to her and said, 'You lovely creature! My wife is dead and when I looked at you, I fell in love with you. So, let me have the pleasure of your company.'

—'My handsome fellow,' she replied, 'if that's the case, I am ready. And what is more, my husband is very rich but so old that he can't even walk. So, we can steal his money, elope together and enjoy life to our heart's content, in another town.'

—'All right then,' said the crook. 'Meet me here early tomorrow morning and we'll go.' The farmer's wife agreed and went home, her face beaming with joy.

"Early in the morning while the old farmer, her husband, was fast asleep, the woman stole all his money, hurried to the rendezvous and met the crook. Then they set out on the journey towards south.

"When they had covered quite some distance, they came to the bank of a river. When the crook saw the river, he thought to himself, 'What is this woman to me! She is at the fag end of her youth. Besides, if somebody follows her and catches up with us, then I am ruined. So what I will do is, rob her and desert her.'

"So, he said to the woman, 'Darling! It's difficult to cross this big river. I will go first with the money and then come back and take you across, on my back.'

—'All right my handsome fellow,' she replied, 'do that then.'

"With this, she handed over to him all her money. When he had collected everything, the rogue said to her, 'Lovely creature, give me the clothes you are wearing too, so that afterwards you can cross the river comfortably.'

"The woman agreed, handed him the clothes and he went off, taking everything with him, and deserted her.

"The woman waited for him on the bank of the river, with her arms crossed over her breasts and her hands on her shoulders.

"Meanwhile, a female jackal arrived on the scene, holding a piece of meat in her mouth. Suddenly a fish leaped out of water and fell on the bank of the river. When the female jackal saw this, she dropped her piece of meat and went to try to catch the fish but somehow the fish managed to slip back into water before she could reach her. So, the female jackal started to return to the place where she had dropped her piece of meat. But meanwhile a vulture swept down, picked up the piece of meat and flew away with it. So the female jackal was looking up at the vulture, full of disappointment, when the woman addressed her with a smile, 'The vulture took your piece of meat away and the fish has gone back into the river. Madam Jackal! You have lost both of them, so what are you staring at?'

"Now the female jackal had seen what had happened between the woman and the crook and had understood that the woman had lost both her husband and her lover. So, she replied, mockingly, 'Naked woman! You are twice as clever as I am, but you have now neither your lover nor your husband, so what are you staring at?'

Now, while the crocodile was telling this story to the monkey, another water-dweller came up and told him, "A bigger crocodile has taken over your house!"

When the crocodile heard this, he was very upset. He pondered over ways and means of driving the other crocodile out. He said to himself, "Oh, look at my

misfortune! My friend has turned into my enemy, my
wife has died and now my house has been occupied by
someone else. What will happen to me next? It is so
true what they say:

> 'You get more cuts where there is already a wound
> And when the food is all gone,
> Then you are more hungry for it.
> During hard times, your enemies multiply.
> All this happens when fate is against you.'

—"Now what shall I do?" went on the crocodile. "Shall
I fight this intruder or persuade him to move out
peacefully? Or shall I bribe him or consult my friend,
the monkey? For they say:

> 'When a man begins a task,
> After consultation with his elders
> And his friends, who wish him well,
> He will never face any hindrance.' "

Then the crocodile spoke to the monkey, who was up
in the Jambu tree, "My dear friend, look at my bad
luck! My house has been occupied by a much bigger
crocodile! So now I am asking you for advice. Tell me,
what shall I do? What tactics shall I adopt: peaceful
negotiation, fighting, bribery or what?"

—"Ungrateful sinner!" said the monkey. "Why are you
running after me although I've forbidden you to? I
won't advise such a rascal as you are!"

—"Please!" said the crocodile. "I know I have done you
wrong but, for the sake of our old friendship, give me
some advice."

—"I will give you no advice!" retorted the monkey. "You
tried to drown me in the sea, just because your wife
prompted you to do so. That was despicable of you. A
wife is dear to us all but you don't drown your friends
just because your wife asks you to. You are doomed to
ruin because you are too stupid to know good advice
when you hear it, for they say:

> 'He who, out of conceit,
> Does not follow the good advice of virtuous people,

Shall certainly be destroyed
As the camel, with a bell round his neck, was by
    the lion.' "
—"How was that?" asked the crocodile.
And the monkey told:

THE STORY OF THE CAMEL WITH A BELL ROUND HIS NECK

"In a certain town, there lived a cart-maker, by the name of Ujjwalaka*. As he got no contracts, he became very poor and he thought to himself, 'To hell with this poverty! All the other people in this town are engaged in one job or the other but I don't get any suitable work. Everybody else owns four-storeyed buildings whilst I don't even have a proper home to live in. What is the use of staying here!'

"And so, the cart-maker and his family left the town to settle somewhere else.

"On the way, whilst they were still deep in the jungle, the sun set. Suddenly, the cart-maker saw a female camel, suffering from labour pains. She had been left behind by a caravan. Soon, she gave birth to a baby camel. The cart-maker tied the female with a rope, fetched a sharp hatchet and went to cut fresh tender leaves for her to eat. He put them in front of her and slowly she started feeding on them.

"Next morning, when the female camel had partly recovered, the cart-maker took her and the baby camel with him to his new home. Under his proper care, the female camel fully recovered and the baby grew to full size. Fondly, the cart-maker tied a bell round the young camel's neck.

"Everyday he would sell the female camel's milk and, in this way, supported his family. Then, he thought to himself, 'Why should I take to any other profession, when I can well support my family merely by looking after camels and selling milk!'

"So, he said to his wife, 'My dear, this business is very profitable. If you agree, I shall borrow some money from somebody wealthy and go to Gujarat* to buy a young female camel. Whilst I am away, please look after these two.' His wife agreed.

"So, the cart-maker went to Gujarat and returned home after buying a young female camel. Fortune smiled on him and, in due course, he was the owner of quite a number of camels. He employed a servant to look after them and paid him one baby camel every year in return for his services. He also gave him free camel milk everyday to drink. And so the cart-maker lived happily, looking after the camels and their young, and subsequently selling them.

"Every morning, the camels would graze in the jungle near by and eat tender creepers and other good things. Then they would go to drink water from a big lake and afterwards return home, playing light-heartedly on the way.

"Now this camel, with a bell round his neck, was conceited and used to trail behind the other camels, all on his own. When the others noticed this, they said, 'This foolish fellow always strays away and walks behind us, with his bell ringing. This makes him very vulnerable. One day he'll get into the clutches of a vicious beast and get himself killed.' They all scolded him about this and tried to make him understand, but he took no notice of them.

"One day, a lion heard the ringing of a bell in the jungle. He followed the sound and saw a caravan of young camels moving ahead. They were going to drink water from a lake. But the one, with a bell round his neck, had strayed behind, all alone and was still grazing. The others finished drinking and started off for home. This camel now began to stray in every direction and he lost his way. The lion followed the sound of the ringing bell, overtook the camel and stood hiding in his path. When the camel came near enough, the lion sprang at him, struck him in the neck and killed him.

—"And so," continued the monkey, "that's why I said:
'He who, out of conceit,
    Does not follow the good advice of virtuous people,
    Shall certainly be destroyed

As the camel, with a bell round his neck, was by
   the lion.' "
When the crocodile heard the story, he said to the
monkey, "Friend! Those well versed in the shastras say:
   'If you walk seven steps together with a man,
   You have become his friend.'
—"So in the name of this friendship of ours, listen to
what I am going to tell you:
   'Those who wish you well
   And give you good advice,
   Shall not lose by it,
   Either in this world or the next.'
—"And so, although I have been ungrateful, please do
give me a bit of advice. As they say:
   'What value has good,
   If it is only good in return for good,
   But when a man returns good for evil,
   He is called great by the wise ones.' "
When the monkey heard this, he said, "Oh, very well
then! If that's the case, I will advise you: Go and fight
him! If you do this, you are benefited either way. If
you get killed, you will go to heaven, but if you win
the fight, you not only have your home back but you
get   other   people's   admiration   as   well.   As
Mahachaturaka*, the jackal, said:
   'Bow before the great,
   Pit two brave opponents against each other,
   Give small presents to the mean,
   And fight with the equally powerful.' "
—"How was that?" asked the crocodile.
And the monkey told:

THE STORY OF THE JACKAL, THE LION, THE LEOPARD AND THE TIGER

"In a certain part of the 3jungle, there lived a jackal, by the name of Mahachaturaka.

"One day, he came across a dead elephant. He went round and round him, trying to tear the elephant's thick skin but he could not.

"Meanwhile, a lion, who was wandering about here and there, arrived on the scene.

"When the jackal saw the lion approaching, he bowed himself low on the ground, joined his paws in obeisance and said very humbly, 'Your Majesty! I am keeping watch over this elephant for you. Now that you have come, please be good enough to eat him.'

"When the lion saw the jackal behaving so humbly, he said, "Thank you very much, but I never eat a prey that has been killed by someone else. As they say:

"A man born of a noble family,
Although beset with calamities,
Never forsakes the path of righteousness:
So too the lion, royal by birth,
Even when faint with hunger,
Never touches grass or animals killed by others."

—'And so,' continued the lion, 'I shall make you a present of this dead elephant.'

—'It's very proper on the master's part,' said the jackal, 'to treat his servants so.'

"After the lion had left, a leopard arrived on the scene. When the jackal saw him, he thought to himself, 'I got rid of the wicked lion by bowing humbly before him, but how shall I manage this one? He is extremely brave, so I cannot handle him except by cunning, for they say:

"When it is not possible
To win someone over by peaceful methods,
Or by bribery,

Then cunning is the only solution,
For even a man endowed with all the good qualities,
Can be won over by cunning.' "

"With this, the jackal raised his shoulders proudly and said condescendingly to the leopard, 'Uncle! Why have you ventured into the jaws of death? The lion killed this elephant, appointed me to watch over him and is now gone to wash himself in the river. When he left, he said to me, "If any leopard turns up, come to me quietly and inform me, I shall then see that this jungle is wiped out of all leopards. For once, one of them polluted my kill of an animal and I have been very angry with leopards ever since." '

"When the leopard heard this, he was frightened and he said, 'Nephew! Please save my life! Don't tell the lion that I've been here.' And with these words, he bolted.

"When the leopard had left, a tiger arrived on the scene. When the jackal saw him, he started thinking, 'He has very strong sharp teeth. I will make him tear open the elephant's hide.'

"With this in mind, he said to the tiger, 'Nephew! How is it that I see you after such a long time? And you look starved. Be my guest. This elephant has been killed by a lion and he ordered me to keep watch over him. But until he returns, eat as much as you can and then leave quickly.'

—'If that's the case,' said the tiger, 'I don't want anything to do with it, for the lion may kill me. They say:
"As long as you manage to stay alive,
There are hundreds of good things to enjoy."
And,
"You should only eat
What you can digest
And what, once digested,
Does you good."
—'And so,' continued the tiger, 'I am leaving!'
—'You coward!' said the jackal. 'Eat and don't worry about it. I'll tell you when the lion is coming back, while

he is still quite a long way off.'

"The tiger was taken in by the jackal's cunning talk. But hardly had he cut through the elephant's hide and taken a few mouthfuls, when the jackal shouted, 'Stop! You had better run, nephew! The lion is coming.' As soon as the tiger heard this, he took to his heels.

"The jackal had just started feeding on the flesh, through the opening made by the tiger, when another jackal arrived on the scene, looking very angry. Guessing that his own strength matched this newcomer's, Mahachaturaka recited to himself the following verse:

'Bow before the great,

Pit two brave opponents against each other,

Give small presents to the mean,

And fight with the equally powerful.' "

"He fought the other jackal, bit him with his sharp teeth and chased him away. And he enjoyed the elephant's flesh all to himself for a long, long time.

—"And so, crocodile," continued the monkey, "don't give your enemy time to entrench himself. You, too, fight off this enemy of your own species, for they say:

'You can expect prosperity from cows,

Penance from Brahmins,

Fickle-mindedness from women

And antagonism from your own kith and kin.'

And another thing, as the dog said:

'In foreign countries, the women are careless

And leave all the doors open,

One gets wonderful varieties of food to eat,

But there is one disadvantage.

Your own kith and kin torment you to death.' "

—"How was that?" asked the crocodile.

And the monkey told:

THE STORY OF THE DOG IN A FOREIGN COUNTRY

"In a certain town, there lived a dog, by the name of Chitranga*. Once, there was famine in the land and, due to lack of food, the dogs along with the other animals began to starve; some even died. Chitranga couldn't put up with such conditions any longer and he left for a foreign country.

"There, in a certain town, because of the negligence of a rich lady householder, he could get into the house everyday and gorge himself on various kinds of food, to his heart's content. But no sooner would he come out, than out of spite, the other dogs would surround him and bite him all over his body with their sharp teeth.

"So then, he thought to himself, 'Oh, it's far better to be in one's own country and live in peace and quiet, in spite of famine! I'm going home!'

And he returned to his own country.

"When he arrived there, his relatives gathered around him and plied him with questions, 'Chitranga! Tell us the news about the foreign land! What is the country like? How did the people behave? What kind of food do they eat? What do they trade in?'

—'What can I say about it?' replied Chitranga. 'In foreign countries, the women are careless and leave all the doors open. One gets wonderful varieties of food to eat. But there is one disadvantage. Your own kith and kin torment you to death.'

When the crocodile heard the monkey's good advice, he made up his mind to fight the other crocodile to the death and, taking leave of his friend, he returned home.

He fought his enemy and killed him. He recovered his home and lived happily ever after.

THE END
OF THE FOURTH TANTRA

ACTION WITHOUT DUE CONSIDERATION

This is the beginning of the fifth tantra called, "Action without due consideration". And here is the first verse:
> "No wise man should follow the barber's example,
> Pursuing what he has neither accurately observed,
> Nor properly understood:
> Neither correctly heard,
> Nor sufficiently considered."

This is how the story goes:

In the south of India, there was a town called Patliputra*. A merchant, by the name of Manibhadra*, lived there. He was given to performing charitable deeds, for the sake of religion, for the love of others, and for the salvation of his soul. But fate was hostile and he lost his entire fortune. As a result, the man's respect and reputation gradually diminished everywhere. He grew utterly dejected.

One night, as he lay in bed, he thought to himself, "Oh, to hell with this poverty! It's so true what they say:
> 'A man may be of good character,
> Compassionate and pure,
> Sweet tempered and born of a noble family,
> But once he has lost his money,
> He is no longer widely esteemed.'

And,
> 'The breeze in spring,
> Gradually diminishes the splendour of winter,
> And the daily cares of maintaining a family,
> Diminish a wise man.'

And,
> 'A poor man's house
> Is like the sky without stars
> Or a lake without water —
> Impressive, but lifeless as a burial ground.'

And,

> 'Poverty-stricken people
> Stand out in their wretchedness
> And yet no one pays them
> Any more attention
> Than bubbles of water
> That form and disappear.'

And,

> 'A poor man may be wise, upright
> And of genteel birth
> But everyone shuns him,
> Whilst a rich man, although stupid, immoral
> And low born,
> Is, for ulterior motives, overwhelmed with attention.'

And also,

> 'The sea roars
> And everyone trembles,
> The rich flaunt themselves
> And are respected by all.' "

Thinking all this over, Manibhadra came to a decision. "What is the good of leading such a useless life?" he said. "I shall fast and starve myself to death."

Then, he dropped off to sleep. He dreamt that a Jain monk appeared to him and said, "Merchant, don't worry! I am Padmanidhi*, accumulated by your forefathers through hard work. Tomorrow morning, I shall come to your house in this very form. Strike me on the head with a stick and I shall turn into gold. You will have so much gold that the supply will never be exhausted."

Early next morning, when the merchant got up, his head was spinning. The memory of the previous night's dream haunted him. He thought to himself, "I wonder whether this dream will come true or not. Very likely it won't. I had this dream because my thoughts were preoccupied with money. It's true what they say:

> 'The dreams of a sick man
> Or a man overcome with grief or worry,
> Desire or madness,

Prophesy nothing.' "

Now, the merchant's wife had called in a barber, to anoint her sore feet and to paint them with Mendi*. Just after his arrival, a Jain monk appeared on the scene. He was the image of the one the merchant had seen in his dream. When the merchant saw him, he was delighted and immediately struck him on the head with a stick that happened to be handy. The monk fell to the ground and turned into a pile of gold!

The merchant picked up the gold and quietly hid it in a secluded room of the house. He made the barber happy by giving him money and clothes, saying to him, "Never tell anybody what you have seen."

When the barber got home, he thought to himself, "Well, if all these Jain monks turn to gold when you hit them on the head, I'll invite a few of them to my house." And he spent a very disturbed night, thinking about it.

Next morning, he got up and went over to the Jain Vihara*. Three times he went round the idol of Jinendra*. Then he knelt on the ground, and holding his upper garment* before his mouth, in the tradition of the Jains, recited the following verse:

"Long live the Jain saints,
For they devote themselves solely
To the pursuit of wisdom.
Lust and desire can no more take root in their minds,
Than green shoots can sprout in the desert.
Blessed is the tongue that praises Mahavira*
And blessed are the hands that minister to him."

When he had finished, the barber went over to the chief monk, knelt on the ground with his hands folded, and said, "Muni*, I bow before you."

In return, the monk blessed him and passed on to him some precepts of the Jain religion. The barber then said very humbly to the chief monk, "Muni, I implore

you, when you go out for alms today, please come and
dine at my house and bring the other monks with you."
—"My good devotee!" said the monk. "You are obviously
a very religious man, so how can you talk like that? Do
you think that we Jains are like Brahmins, that you've
come to invite us to your home to eat! Don't you know
that when we go out collecting alms everyday, we accept
food from the first devotee we come across and then
only eat just enough to keep ourselves alive? So, go
away and don't talk like that again."
—"But, Muni," said the barber, "I know your religion
quite well and I also know that you do accept invitations
from devotees. Now, I have collected a number of
exquisite pieces of cloth, which would be beautiful to
wrap round your holy books. I have also saved a lot of
money to give to the scribes who copy them. But please,
don't let this influence you, do as you think best."

Then the barber asked for the chief monk's blessings
and went home.

When he got there, he put a stick, made of Khadira*
wood, behind the door, in readiness. Then at lunch
time, he went back to the Vihara and waited outside.

When the monks came out, he begged them to
accompany him to his house to conduct prayers. Coveting
the cloth and the money, the monks agreed and went
with the barber. As they say:

"Isn't it amazing!
Even a recluse
Who has given up his home,
Discarded his utensils,
And now eats and drinks with his bare hands,
Is a prey to greed."
And,
"An old man's hair turn white,
His teeth grow loose
And his eyes and ears cease to function properly,
But his desires remain eternally young."

As soon as the monks entered the barber's house, he locked the doors firmly from inside and began to beat them on their heads, with the stick. Some fell down dead, some had their heads smashed in, whilst the others began to scream for help.

When the chief watchman of the town heard their cries, he ordered his men to go and find out what all this noise was about, right in the centre of the town. The watchmen went to look and they saw the monks rushing out of the barber's house with blood streaming from them.

—"Whatever has happened?" they asked the monks. And the monks told them all that the barber had done. The watchmen arrested the barber and took him to the court of law, and the monks as well.

At court, the judges said to the barber, "Why did you commit this wicked crime?"

—"It wasn't my fault!" he said. "I saw the merchant do it. And I thought, I too would try." And he told them all that he had seen at Manibhadra's house.

Then the judges ordered the merchant to appear before them and they asked him, "Have you been killing any Jain monks?"

The merchant told them in detail all about the monk in his dream.

Then the judges said, "Let this wicked barber, who blindly imitated the merchant, be put to death." And the barber was hanged.

Then the judges said,

> "No wise man should follow the barber's example,
> Pursuing what he has neither accurately observed,
> Nor properly understood,
> Neither correctly heard
> Nor sufficiently considered."

And,

> "He who acts without due consideration,
> Will afterwards repent,

As the Brahmin's wife repented
The death of the mongoose."
—"How was that?" asked the merchant.
And the judges told:

THE STORY OF THE BRAHMIN'S WIFE AND
THE MONGOOSE

"In a certain town, there lived a Brahmin, by the name of Dev Sharma*. One day, his wife gave birth to a son. The very same day, a female mongoose gave birth to a baby mongoose, but she herself died.

"Out of compassion, the Brahmin's wife took the little mongoose and brought him up as her own son, giving him her own breast milk and bathing him in oil. However, she was always on her guard, thinking to herself, 'This mongoose has inherited the defects of his species and may some day harm my son.' She was a very fond mother. As they say:

"A son may be useless, conceited,

Ugly, stupid, badly behaved or wicked,

His parents will still dote on him."

"One day, the woman put her son to bed and then wanted to take her pitcher to fetch water. So she said to her husband, 'I'm going to the well to fetch water. Look after the baby and make sure the mongoose doesn't hurt him.'

"But after she had gone, the Brahmin also left the house and went to beg alms. Meanwhile, a black snake emerged from a hole. To defend the child, who was like a brother to him, the mongoose attacked his natural enemy, fought with him, bit him to pieces and killed him. His mouth and claws were all spattered with the snake's blood. Then, in his eagerness to show how brave he had been, the mongoose went and stood outside the house, waiting for the Brahmin's wife.

"But when she arrived and saw him covered with blood, the woman jumped to the conclusion that he had killed her son. She brought the heavy pitcher, full of water, down heavily on the mongoose and killed him on the spot.

"When she went inside, she found her child safe in

his cradle, and a black snake, torn to shreds, lying near by. She was heart-broken. She felt as though she had been guilty of killing her own son and she began to beat her breasts in self-reproach.

"After some time, the Brahmin returned home. 'Damn you!' cried his grief-stricken wife. 'Greedy fellow! You were so anxious for alms that you didn't listen to me. Now repent the loss of your second son, eat the fruit of your greed. It's so true what they say:

"Be ambitious, within limits,
    For when a man is too greedy,
    A wheel whirls around his head:
    That's what happened to Chakradhara* "
—'How was that?' asked the Brahmin.
And his wife told:

THE STORY OF CHAKRADHARA

" 'In a certain town, there lived four young fellows, who were the sons of Brahmins. They were very friendly with each other. But they were utterly destitute, so they met to decide what to do. "Curse this poverty," they said. "It's so true what they say:

'When a man loses his money,
His friends and relatives avoid him,
He is deserted by his own sons.
Even a gentle wife, born of good family,
Wants nothing to do with him.
None of his good qualities are appreciated
And his troubles multiply.
His name, his body, his voice, his mind.
Remain the same
But everything else collapses in a flash.'
And,
'It is much better to live in seclusion,
In a thorny jungle, full of tigers and elephants,
To sleep on a bed of grass and wear clothes made
of bark,
Than to live, amongst one's kith and kin, in utter
poverty.'
—"And so," concluded the four friends, "Let us leave this town and go somewhere else."

" 'Then they gave up their home, their town, their friends and their relatives and started off on their travels.

" 'After some time, they came to Avanti*. They bathed in the river Sipra* and worshipped at Shiva's temple. As they were coming out, they met a Yogi, by the name of Bhairavananda*. They bowed respectfully to him and accompanied him to his ashrama.

" 'When they arrived there, he asked them, "Who are you? Where do you come from? And where are you going? What is the purpose of your journey?"
—"We are going where we can either make money or

meet our death," they said. "For they say:
   'Water comes
   Not only in the form of rain,
   Dropped from the sky,
   But also by digging deep in the earth.'
—"Now we have heard that you are gifted with
wonderful powers. So please tell us some way of making
money, whether it be by going into a cave, living in a
Smashana*, by praying to Shakini*, by offering human
sacrifices, or with the help of magic wicks*. Please help
us."

" 'Bhairavananda took pity on them and gave them
four wicks, made of cotton, one to each of them, and
said, "Go in the direction of the Himalayas. When any
one of you accidentally drops his wick, you will be sure
to find a treasure hidden in that spot. Dig it out, collect
the treasure and return home with it."

" 'The four Brahmins nodded their consent and started
off towards the Himalayas.

" 'After a few days' journey, one of them dropped his
cotton wick. He dug where it had fallen and uncovered
a treasure of copper. He began to collect the copper
and cried to the others, "Come on, you too take as
much as you can carry and let's go home. Why go any
further!"

—"Stupid!" replied the others. "However much copper
you collect, you will still be poor. Let us go on."

—"Well," he replied, "you can go on but I shall return
home with this copper." And so, he took as much copper
as he could carry and returned home. The other three
continued their journey.

" 'After a few days, the second Brahmin dropped his
cotton wick. He started digging and uncovered a treasure
of silver. He cried out in delight and said to the other
two, "Come on, you too take as much as you can carry
and let's go home. Why go any further!"

—"Stupid!" replied the others. "However much silver
you collect, you'll still be relatively poor. Besides, first

we had copper and now we have silver. Next time we
are sure to find gold. So let us go on."

—"You can go on," he replied, "but I shall return home
with this silver." And so, he collected as much silver as
he could carry and returned home. The other two
continued their journey.

" 'After a few days, the third Brahmin dropped his
cotton wick. Joyfully, he started digging in the ground
and he uncovered a heap of gold. "Come on," he cried
to his companion, "you too take as much gold as you
can carry and let's go home. Why go any further!"

—"Stupid!" replied the other. "You don't understand
anything. First it was copper, then silver and now gold.
Next time, we're sure to find diamonds and pearls, so
that if we take only one, we shall never be poor again.
In any case, what is the point of carrying all this heavy
load? Let us go on."

—"You can go on," replied his companion, "but I shall
stay here and watch over this gold. I'll wait until you
return." So, the fourth Brahmin continued his journey
alone.

" 'When he had gone some way, the fourth Brahmin
began to suffer from the tremendous heat and he felt
very thirsty. Soon, he lost the way that the Yogi had
directed him to follow, and began to go round and
round in circles. While he was wandering, he suddenly
came across a man, whose body was smeared all over
with blood. The man had a wheel whirling around his
head. Quickly the Brahmin went over to him and said,
"Who are you and what is this wheel around your head?
But whoever you are, for goodness sake, tell me quickly
where can I get water?"

" 'Now, the minute he uttered these words, the wheel
shifted from the other man to him and began to whirl
around his own head. "Friend!" he cried. "What is this?"

—"This wheel attached itself to my head in similar
circumstances," replied the man.

—"But when shall I get rid of it?" wailed the Brahmin.

"It pains me beyond endurance!"

—"Only when someone carrying a magic wick comes here and speaks to you," replied the man, "will this wheel leave you and attach itself to him."

—"How long have you been here?" asked the Brahmin.

" 'By way of reply, the man asked him, "Who is ruling the earth now?"

—"Veenavaunsha*," replied the Brahmin.

—"I cannot guess accurately when I came here," said the man. "But I remember that it was in the reign of King Rama* that I was desperate with poverty. I managed to procure a magic wick and in due course, ended up here. I saw a man with a wheel whirling around his head. I asked him the same questions you asked me and, in the same way, the wheel left him and attached itself to me."

—"But friend," said the Brahmin, "how did you manage to get food and water, with a wheel whirling around your head all the time?"

—"My dear fellow," replied the man, "anyone who comes here is free from hunger, thirst, old age and death, but he suffers pain all the time, as you do now. Kuber*, afraid that his treasure would be stolen, prepared this device and ever since no one dare approach this place, except with the help of a magic wick. Now, good-bye. I am going home."

" 'With these words, the man took his leave and left the Brahmin alone.

" 'Now, when the Brahmin's friend, whose name was Suvaranasiddhi*, found that he was taking so long to return, he followed his footprints and finally arrived at the same place. He found his friend drenched in blood, his eyes flooding with tears and a wheel whirling around his head. "Friend," he said, "whatever has happened?"

—"It's all the result of fate being against me!" replied Chakradhara. And he told him the whole story of the whirling wheel. When he had finished, his friend said, "Brother, you are a good scholar, but you lack

commonsense. You would not listen to my good advice
when I said, 'Let's pick up the gold and go home.' You
wanted pearls and diamonds. Well, it's true what they
say:

    'Commonsense is superior to scholarship:
    The scholars who were devoid of commonsense,
    Put life into the lion and died as a result.' "
—"How was that?" asked Chakradhara.
And Suvaranasiddhi told:

THE STORY OF THE BRAHMINS WHO PUT LIFE INTO THE LION

" ' "In a certain town, there lived f3our sons of Brahmins. They were great friends. Three of them were very well versed in the shastras, but lacking in commonsense. The fourth was completely ignorant of the shastras, but had good commonsense.

" ' "One day, these four friends had a discussion together. They said, 'What is the good of scholarship, if you cannot impress kings in far off lands by it, or earn money with it? So, let us travel east.'

" ' "Accordingly, they set out. When they had covered some distance, the eldest of them said, 'One of us has only commonsense and no scholarship. Now, no one earns the king's esteem by mere commonsense, so let us not give him any of our share of the profits. In fact, let him go home.'

" ' "The second Brahmin turned to the one with commonsense and said to him, 'My friend, you are no scholar, so you had better go home.'

" ' "But the third one said, 'We shouldn't behave like this towards our friend. After all, we have grown up together and played games with one another since we were children. So let him come. What's more, he should get his share of our earnings, for they say:

"A mean-minded man
Thinks, 'This is mine, and that is his,'
But to a generous man,
The whole world is one big family." '

" ' "Finally, the others agreed and they all proceeded on their way. After some time, they came to a jungle and found the bones of a lion lying there. Then one of them suggested, 'Let's put our scholarship to test. Here lies a dead lion. We'll see if we can bring him to life.'

" ' "And so, one of them collected bones and made

a skeleton of them. The second one put flesh and blood
into it, covering it with skin. The third one was on the
point of putting the very life back into the lion, when
the fourth restrained him, 'Stop friend!' he cried. 'For
goodness sake, don't do that! Look here, if you bring
this dead lion to life, he'll kill the whole lot of us!'

" ' "But the third Brahmin shouted, 'You don't think
I am going to waste all my learning, after we've got so
far, do you?'

—'All right then,' said the fellow with commonsense,
'but just wait a minute, while I climb up this tree.' And
off he went up the tree.

" ' "The third Brahmin brought the lion to life. The
lion immediately set on the three of them and killed
them. The one with the commonsense waited until the
lion had gone, then he got down from the tree and
went home.

—"And so," continued Suvaranasiddhi, "that's why I
said,

'Commonsense is superior to scholarship:
The scholars who were devoid of commonsense,
Put life into the lion and died as a result.'

—"They also say," he continued,

'People well versed in the shastras,
But lacking in commonsense,
Become the object of ridicule,
Like the four learned fools.' "

—"How was that?" asked Chakradhara.
And Suvaranasiddhi told:

THE STORY OF THE FOUR LEARNED FOOLS

" ' "In a certain town, there lived four Brahmins who had become great friends. They were all extremely naive by nature. One day, they said to each other, 'Let us all go to another kingdom, study hard and then make some money there.' So, they set off for Kanyakubja* to get their education. They joined an ashrama and began a course of study.

" ' "They worked hard at this ashrama for twelve years. Then, one day, they said to each other, 'We have now acquired sufficient knowledge in all branches of the sciences. Let us go to our Guru*, get his permission and leave.' So, they did this and left the ashrama, taking all their shastras with them.

" ' "After they had been travelling for a short time, they came to a place where two paths met. They stood still and pondered. One of them said, 'Which way shall we go?'

" ' "Now, the son of a merchant had died in the town and, at this very moment, a huge funeral procession, including several prominent citizens of the town, passed by, on its way to the Smashana.

" ' "Then one of the Brahmins consulted his shastras and read.

'Whichever road is followed by great men,
Is the right one to follow.'

" ' "So they said, 'Let us go the same way as these people.' And they started following the road taken by the prominent citizens.

" ' "When they reached the Smashana, they saw a donkey standing there. As they could not decide what to do next, the second Brahmin consulted his shastras and read.

'Whosoever stands by you on a joyful occasion,
In calamity, sickness, famine or war,
In the court of law or at the Smashana,

Is your true friend.'

" ' "And so, one of the Brahmins put his arms round the donkey's neck, the second kissed him, whilst the third began to wash his hoofs. 'For,' they said, 'he is our true friend!'

" ' "Meanwhile, they saw, in the distance, a camel coming quickly towards them. The third Brahmin consulted his shastras and read.

'Righteousness marches rapidly.'

" ' "So they all decided that this camel must be nothing but righteousness incarnate.

" ' "Then the fourth Brahmin opened his shastras and read,

'A wise man should lead his friend to righteousness.'

" ' "And so, they decided that the donkey should be introduced to the camel, and when the camel approached, they tied them up together.

" ' "When the donkey's master, a washerman, heard the news that his donkey was being dragged along by a camel, he picked up a stick and ran after the four learned fools to beat them. And they ran for their lives.

" ' "When they had gone a little way, they came to a river. The leaf of a Palasha* tree was floating by. One of them cried, 'This floating leaf will take us across the river.' And with this, he jumped on it and immediately began to drown. The second Brahmin grabbed him by the hair and remembered a quotation from the shastras,

'When total destruction is imminent,

A wise man sacrifices half

And works with the rest,

For a complete loss is unbearable.'

—'So,' he concluded, 'he should be cut in two!' And they cut him in two halves with a sharp sword.

" ' "The three remaining Brahmins wandered on, until they reached a village. There, they were invited by the villagers and lodged in different houses.

" ' "One of the Brahmins was served with sweet Sutrika*. When he saw the long noodles-like substance, he remembered the verse that says,

'A man who makes use of long tactics,
Is sure to be destroyed.'

" ' "So, he did not touch the food and went away hungry.

" ' "The second Brahmin was served with Mandaka*. When he saw the bowl of frothy food, he remembered the verse that says,

'Whatever is frothy and distended,
Will not last long.'

" ' "So, he too left his food and went away hungry.

" ' "The third Brahmin was given a Vatika*. When he saw all the little holes in it, he remembered the verse that says,

'The presence of defects,
Is a sure sign of approaching disaster.'

" ' "So, he too left his food and went away hungry.

" ' "Thus, the three learned fools began to starve and started out on their journey home, with all and sundry ridiculing them on the way.

—"And so," continued Suvaranasiddhi, "that's why I said,

'People well versed in the shastras,
But lacking in commonsense,
Become the object of ridicule,
Like the four learned fools.'

—"You too, Chakradhara, are devoid of commonsense. You would not listen to me. That's why you have been reduced to this state."

—"But that's not the reason," said Chakradhara. "It's because fate is against me. As they say:

'An orphan whom fortune smiles on,
Though left unprotected in a jungle, survives,
But a man with luck against him,
Even though he is well protected,
Dies in his own home.'

And,

'When fate is hostile,

Even the talented pay with their lives,
Whilst those with lesser talents live happily.'
As the frog said,
'The fisherman is carrying
Sahasrabuddhi*, with his thousand talents, on his head,
And Shatabuddhi*, with his hundred talents,
Is hanging from his hand,
Whilst I, Ekabuddhi*, with my single talent, am swimming happily in this water.' "
—"How was that?" asked Suvaranasiddhi.
And Chakradhara told:

THE STORY OF TWO FISHES AND THE FROG

" ' "In a certain pond, there lived two fishes. Their names were Shatabudhi and Sahasrabuddhi. They had made friends with a frog by the name of Ekabuddhi. The three of them used to spend their time together, on the bank of the pond, conversing about philosophy.

" ' "One evening, while they were thus engaged in conversation, some fishermen passed by, carrying baskets of fish on their heads and nets in their hands. When they came to the pond, they said to one another, 'This pond seems to be full of fishes and, besides, the water is not very deep. Let's come here tomorrow morning and throw our nets.' With these words, they continued on their way home.

" ' "When the fishes and the frog heard this, they were very depressed and held a discussion together.

—'Friends,' said the frog, 'did you hear what the fishermen said? What shall we do? Should we run away or stay on?'

" ' "Sahasrabuddhi laughed and said, 'My dear fellow, don't be frightened by mere talk! They say:

"If the wishes of snakes, rogues and wicked people
  Were fulfilled,
The world would come to an end."

—'To begin with, I don't expect they will come. But even if they do, I shall protect you with my thousand talents, for I know innumerable tricks of movement in the water.'

—'Friend,' said Shatabuddhi, 'you have spoken very convincingly. I know you have a thousand talents. I myself have a hundred talents. As they say:

"Nothing in life is impossible,
  For talented people,
Chanakya* killed the heavily armed members of
  the Nanda* family,
Without the use of any weapons."

—'So, we whould not abandon our place of birth, the home of our ancestors, for the sake of mere talk.'

" ' "When he heard this, the frog said, 'Well, my friends, I have only one talent, the ability to foresee, and it counsels me to go away. I am leaving with my wife for some other pond this very night.'

" ' "Accordingly, the frog left the pond. Next morning, the fishermen arrived, cast their nets and caught all types of water-dwellers, large and small fishes, tortoises, frogs and crabs. Shatabuddhi, Sahasrabuddhi and their wives tried to escape, by making use of their talents in manoeuvre, but all in vain. They were caught in the net and died.

" ' "At midday, the fishermen started off joyously for home. As Sahasrabuddhi was heavy, he was carried on a fisherman's head, whilst Shatabuddhi was hanging from his hand.

" ' "The frog had taken shelter in a well. He came to the surface and saw the fishes being carried by the fishermen. He turned to his wife and said, 'My dear, look! The fisherman is carrying Sahasrabuddhi, with his thousand talents, on his head, and Shatabuddhi, with his hundred talents, is hanging from his hand, whilst I, Ekabuddhi, with my single talent, am swimming happily in this water.

—"And so," continued Chakradhara, "that's why I said, that even clever people are helpless when fate is against them."

—"But you should not have turned a deaf ear to a friend's advice," said Suvaranasiddhi. "As the jackal said to the donkey:

'Uncle! What a song!

I asked you not to sing

But you refused to listen.

This exquisite necklace is your reward for sing-ing!' "

—"How was that?" said Chakradhara.

And Suvaranasiddhi told:

THE STORY OF THE SINGING DONKEY

" ' "In a certain town, there lived a donkey, by the name of Uddhata*. He belonged to a washerman. During the daytime, he carried the washerman's heavy loads, whilst at night, he was allowed to wander as he liked, across the fields. But every morning, the donkey would return to the washerman on time — he was afraid that if he failed to, the washerman would keep him tied up all night.

" ' "One night, while the donkey was wandering about in the fields, he met a jackal and got friendly with him. Now, the donkey, being fat, could break down the hedges, and he and the jackal used to get into the cucumber fields. Whilst the donkey was gorging himself on the cucumbers, the jackal would eat poultry from the nearby farm. Then, in the morning, they would return to their respective homes.

" ' "One particular night, the donkey was standing in the middle of the cucumber fields, when he suddenly said to the jackal, 'Nephew, look! Look at the full moon and the beautiful cloudless night! I feel like singing. Tell me, what Raga* shall I sing?'

—'Uncle,' replied the jackal, 'you have come to steal and you'll only be asking for trouble if you sing. Thieves should always stay quiet, for they say:
"A man who has a cough,
   Or is in a habit of dozing off,
   Shouldn't take to stealing."
And,
"A man who is sick,
   Shouldn't take to gluttony."
—'Besides, your singing isn't all that pleasant. It sounds as though somebody is blowing a conch! And you can be heard a long way off. The farmers are sleeping. If you wake them, they'll come out and beat us. So, eat some of these nectareous cucumbers and give up the

idea of singing.'

" ' "When the donkey heard this, he said, 'My dear nephew, you're a wild animal. You don't appreciate the value of music. That's why you talk like that. You know, they say:

"Blessed is he who listens to sweet music,
    With his beloved beside him
    And the autumn moon shining overhead,
    Dispelling the darkness." '

—'That's very true, uncle,' said the jackal, 'but you don't know how to sing. You only know how to bray. And what is the good of such singing, when it will only bring disaster?'

—'Go on!' said the donkey. 'You say that I don't know how to sing, but I know all the systems underlying musical composition. Listen: according to Bharatamuni*, music consists of seven notes, three scales, twenty-one modulations, forty-nine rhythms and three speeds. There are also several Ragas and Raginis* which have to be sung at the proper time and season. Now! How can you say, after all this, that I don't know anything about singing!'

—'Uncle,' said the jackal, 'if you're so determined to sing, I'll stay outside the hedge and be on the lookout for the farmers. Then, you can sing to your heart's content.' And the jackal hid himself behind the hedge.

" ' "Now when the farmers heard the donkey braying, they clenched their teeth angrily and ran to the spot, with sticks in their hands. When they saw the donkey, they beat him so hard that he fell to the ground. Then they picked up a wooden mortar, with no bottom in it, and tied it to the donkey's neck with a rope. Then they returned to their quarters and went back to sleep.

" ' "As is usual with this species, the donkey soon forgot his pain and got up. They say:

'With a dog, a horse and particularly a donkey,
    The pain caused by beating does not last long.'

" ' "When the donkey jumped over the hedge, with

the wooden mortar hanging from his neck, the jackal saw him and said with a smile 'Uncle! What a song! I asked you not to sing, but you refused to listen. This exquisite necklace is your reward for singing!'

—"And so," continued Suvaranasiddhi, "that's why I said, that you shouldn't have turned a deaf ear to a friend's advice."

—"That's true," said Chakradhara, "for they say:
'He who neither has commonsense,
Nor listens to what his friends tell him,
Is sure to be destroyed,
Like Mantharaka*, the weaver.' "

—"How was that?" asked Suvaranasiddhi.

And Chakradhara told:

THE STORY OF MANTHARAKA, THE WEAVER

" ' "In a certain town, there lived a weaver, by the name of Mantharaka. One day, while he was weaving, the wooden supports of the loom broke. So, he took an axe with him and went to the jungle to cut wood.

" ' "While he was wandering on the sea-shore, he came across a giant Shinvshapa tree, and he thought to himself, 'This is a very big tree. If I cut it down, I shall be able to make many looms out of it.' So, he started hacking at the tree with the axe.

" ' "Now, in this tree lived a Devata*. He called out to the weaver, 'Weaver! Stop! This tree is my home, so please spare it. The cool breeze, coming in from the sea, blows against this tree and I live here very happily.' —'What am I to do?' said the weaver. 'If I have no wood to make a loom, my family will die of starvation. So, I have to cut this tree down. You'll have to find somewhere else to live.'

— 'My son,' replied the Devata, 'you have answered well. I am pleased with you. Ask for any boon you like and I will grant it, but spare this tree.'

— 'Well,' replied the weaver, 'if that's the case. I'll go home, consult my wife and friends, and come back. Then I'll tell you what I want and you can give it to me.'

— 'All right,' said the Devata, 'do that.'

" ' "On his return to the town, the weaver met his friend, a barber. He said to him, 'My friend, a Devata is pleased with me and he has said that I can ask any boon of him and he will grant it. I have come back for some advice.'

— 'If I were you,' said the barber, 'I would ask for a kingdom. Then you can be the king and I'll be your prime minister. We can spend a happy life here and afterwards enjoy life in the next world.'

— 'Well,' said the weaver, 'that sounds all right, but I

must go and consult my wife as well.'

— 'Don't do that!' said the barber. 'The shastras advise against consulting women, for their intelligence is of a lower calibre than ours. The shastras state that:

"A wise man should give his woman,
Food, clothes and ornaments,
And have children by her,
But he should never consult her on matters of importance."

And Shukracharaya* has said:

"A house ruled by a woman,
An addict or a child,
Is sure to be destroyed." '

— 'Nevertheless,' replied the weaver, 'I must consult my wife. She is faithful and devoted. I never do anything without consulting her.'

" ' "And so, the weaver hurried home and said to his wife, 'My dear, a Devata is pleased with me. He said that I can ask any boon of him and he will grant it. So, I have come home to consult you. My friend, the barber, has advised me to ask for a kingdom.'

— 'Fancy asking a barber's advice!' retorted his wife. 'Don't listen to him! Besides, they say:

"It is difficult to rule a kingdom:
There is always some trouble or the other
Which robs a king of his peace.
For the sake of a kingdom,
Rama* had to take to the jungle,
The Pandavas* were exiled,
The Yadavas* were slaughtered,
King Nala* was dethroned,
Arjuna* almost fell in the jaws of death
And Ravana* was destroyed.
So, no wise man covets a kingdom,
For whose sake, brothers, sons and close relatives,
Plot to take each other's lives." '

— 'You have spoken wisely,' replied the weaver. 'Now tell me, what shall I ask for?'

— 'Well,' she replied, 'we can meet our expenses with the one piece of cloth you weave everyday. So, you had better ask for two more hands and another head, so that you can make two pieces of cloth, one in front and one behind. Then, by selling one piece, you can live as comfortably as before and with the money from the second piece, you can perform good deeds. In this way, you will earn esteem among your relatives and, at the same time, a place in the heaven.'

" ' "When the weaver heard this, he was delighted and said, 'Well, my faithful wife! How wisely you have spoken. I shall act accordingly. I have made my decision.'

" ' "And so, the weaver returned to the sea-shore and prayed to the Devata, 'Devata, if you will grant me a boon, then give me two more hands and an extra head.' He had no sooner spoken than his wish was granted.

" ' "As the weaver was going home, full of joy, the town people saw him and thought that it was a monster. They threw sticks and stones at him and killed him.

— "And so," continued Chakradhara, "that's why I said:

'He who neither has commonsense.
Nor listens to what his friends tell him,
Is sure to be destroyed,
Like Mantharaka, the weaver.'

— "But then, anyone who comes into contact with the devil, in the form of greed, ultimately becomes an object of ridicule. They say:

'When a man hankers after things,
That are impossible to achieve,
Or may never happen,
He comes to grief,
Like Soma Sharma's* father.' "

— "How was that?" asked Suvaranasiddhi.
And Chakradhara told:

THE STORY OF SOMA SHARMA'S FATHER

" ' "In a certain village, there lived a Brahmin, by the name of Swabhavakripana.* He used to live by begging. Whenever he got wheat flour, he would eat a small portion of it and collect what was left in a pot which he had hung up on a peg, at the foot of his bed and used to stare at the pot, while he was going off to sleep. One night, he was staring at the pot, when he thought to himself, 'This pot is now completely full of wheat flour. If famine comes, I shall be able to make quite a bit of money out of it. Then, I can buy two goats. Now, goats bear kids every six months, so, in due course, I shall have a vast flock of goats. When there are enough, I'll sell them and buy cows. By selling the cows, I shall buy buffaloes, and by selling the buffaloes, I shall buy mares and they will bear me many horses. When I sell the horses, I shall have a lot of gold. With this money, I shall buy a house with four storeys. Then some Brahmin will come and offer me his beautiful young daughter. I shall marry her and she will bear me a son, and I shall call him Soma Sharma. When he is old enough to crawl, I shall take a book to the stable and read. Soma Sharma will get off his mother's lap and crawl after me, beside the horses' hoofs. I'll shout to his mother, "Hey! Come and take this child away!" She being busy with the household chores, won't take any notice. I shall get angry, get up, go across to her and give her a kick.' With this day dreaming, he gave such a kick to his flour pot that it smashed and the wheat flour came flowing down, enveloping him in white.

— "And so," continued Chakradhara,
'When a man hankers after things,
That are impossible to achieve,
Or may never happen,
He comes to grief,
Like Soma Sharma's father.' "

— "Well, actually, you are not to be blamed for what
has happened," said Suvaranasiddhi. "When someone
gets entangled in greed, he has to pay for it. It's true
what they say:

    'A man who, overcome with greed,
      Does not think about the consequences,
      Will be put to scorn like King Chandra*.' "

— "How was that?" asked Chakradhara.

And Suvaranasiddhi told:

THE STORY OF KING CHANDRA

" ' "In a certain city, there lived a king, by the name of Chandra. His sons kept a troop of monkeys. They always fed them on a variety of choice foods and the monkeys had become fat.

" ' "The chief of the monkeys was a follower of the philosophy of Shukra, Brihaspati and Chanakya. Not only did he follow them himself, but also he was always advising others to do so.

" ' "Now, at the palace, there was also a pair of rams, who used to draw the carriage for the young princes. One of the rams was a glutton and he would go into the kitchen at all odd hours and take whatever food he could find there. The cooks would get mad at him and hit him with anything they had handy — sticks, earthenware pots, copper pans and so on, and chase him out.

" ' "When the chief of the monkeys noticed this, his intuition told him: 'This quarrel, between the cooks and the ram, is going to lead to the destruction of the monkeys. This ram craves for food, runs into the kitchen and makes the cooks mad. They hit him with anything they happen to have handy. One day, when they can't find anything else, they'll hit him with a piece of burning wood. The ram is covered with wool and it will easily catch fire. Blazing, he may well rush into the stable, which is full of dry grass, and set that on fire. Then the horses will be burnt. Now, Shalihotra* has said:

"As the darkness is dispelled by the rising sun,
So, wounds caused by fire, disappear
When monkey fat is applied to them."

— 'And that will be the end of the monkeys! Somehow, I have premonition that it will all eventually happen like this.'

" ' "And so, the monkey chief called all the monkeys to him and told them, 'This quarrel, between the cooks

and the ram, is going to have repercussions on us,
monkeys! Anyone who wants to stay alive, should leave
this palace immediately. As they say:

"Because of quarrels,
Beautiful palaces get destroyed,
Due to harsh words,
Friendships come to an end
And due to the evil actions of its king,
A whole nation is annihilated."

—'So, let us leave this palace, before we are all destroyed.'

" ' "But the crazy monkeys paid no attention to him.
They merely laughed and said, 'You're getting old and
going a bit off your head! That's why you talk like this.
We shall certainly not leave this heavenly palace where
the princes feed us, with their own hands, on all kinds
of nectareous foods. In the jungle, all we shall get, will
be disgusting fruits — bitter, raw or over-ripe.'

" ' "When he heard this, with tears in his eyes, the
monkey chief said, 'You fools! You don't understand
what this happy life will lead you to. This tasty food
will, in the end, become poison. I don't want to see the
destruction of my own tribe before my very eyes, so I
am leaving for the jungle. They say:

"Blessed is he who does not see a friend in distress,
Or calamity in the house
And the ruination of his family and land." '

" ' "Then, the chief of the monkeys gave up everything
and went to the jungle.

" ' "One day, shortly after, the ram entered the kitchen
again. A cook, unable to lay hands on anything else,
picked up a half-burnt log and struck the ram with it.
The ram's body, being covered with wool, started blazing
and he rushed into the stable, bleating. He rolled on a
heap of grass lying there and it immediately caught fire,
and soon the flames were enveloping everything around.
Some of the horses were burnt to death, some lost their
eyes, some, half-burnt, broke free from the ropes and
began to dash about in great panic. There was

pandemonium.

" ' "The king was very distressed when he heard the news. He assembled his veterinary surgeons and said to them, 'Please prescribe some remedy to heal the horses' wounds, caused by the burns.'

" ' "The veterinary surgeons referred to the shastras and said, 'Your Majesty, in this connection, the great Shalihotra has said,

"As the darkness is dispelled by the rising sun,
So, wounds caused by fire, disappear
When monkey fat is applied to them."

— 'So, we advise you to make use of this remedy, before the horses die of the burns.'

" ' "And so, the king ordered the massacre of the monkeys. The people killed them all with sticks and anything else that came to hand.

" ' "When the monkey chief heard about the dreadful death of his brothers, sons, nephews, grandsons and the rest of them, he was heart-broken. He gave up eating and began to wander from one part of the jungle to another. He thought to himself, 'How can I make this king pay for this wicked deed, for they say:

"He who, from fear or self-interest,
Lets an insult go unavenged,
Is indeed a man of little worth.' "

" ' "One day, the monkey chief, in the course of his wanderings, felt thirsty and came to a lake full of beautiful lotus blossoms. Now, being observant, he noticed that the footsteps of men and animals were going towards the lake but none were to be seen returning. So, he began to think, 'There must be a hideous monster in the lake who drags them in, while they're drinking water. I will fetch the hollow stem of a lotus plant and drink from a safe distance.' So, that is what he did.

" ' "While he was drinking, out from the lake emerged a Rakshasa, with a necklace of jewels around his neck. 'Ho, you!' he cried to the monkey. 'I feed on whoever enters the lake. But I have never seen anyone as shrewd as you, for you are drinking water without coming in. I am pleased with you. You can ask for whatever you like and I will grant it to you.'

— 'Thank you,' replied the monkey chief, 'but first, please tell me, how many people can you eat at one time?'

— 'I can eat hundreds, thousands and even millions,' replied the Rakshasa, 'but they have to enter the lake. Outside it, I can't touch even a jackal.'

— 'You see,' said the monkey chief, 'I have a great enmity with a certain king. Now, if you give me that necklace of yours, I promise to persuade the king and his court to enter the lake.'

" ' "The Rakshasa took the monkey at his word and handed over his necklace, saying, 'I'll leave it all to you.'

" ' "The monkey chief put the necklace around his neck and swung from tree to tree, until he came to King Chandra's city.

" ' "When the people saw him dressed up like this, they said, 'Monkey Chief! Where have you been all this time! And where did you get this necklace? Its splendour puts even the sun to shame.'

— 'Kuber gave it to me,' replied the monkey chief. 'He has secretly made a lake in the jungle. And whoever takes a bath in the lake on a Sunday, when the sun has just half risen, gets a diamond necklace around his neck and the blessings of the God.'

" ' "Finally, the king too came to hear of this. He called the monkey chief and asked him, 'Monkey Chief, does this lake full of diamond necklaces really exist?'

— 'Your Majesty,' said the monkey, 'this necklace, adorning my neck, is a positive proof of it. If you want one, come with me and I'll show you the lake.'

— 'In that case,' said the king, 'I'll come personally and bring my entire court with me, so that we can have many of the necklaces.'

— 'Please do,' said the monkey chief.

" ' "And so, greedy for diamonds, everyone in the
king's household, his wives, servants, ministers and
everybody else started off. The monkey chief was fondly
put in the king's lap, and stroked and patted. It's true
what the say:

'Avarice, I bow to you,
You make men do things,
They ought not have done,
And wander in places
Where they ought not have gone.
He who has a hundred,
Wants a thousand;
He who has a thousand,
Wants a hundred thousand;
He who has a hundred thousand,
Wants millions;
And a king covets the kingdom of the heaven.'

And,

'In old age, the hair turn white,
The teeth become loose,
The eyes and the ears cease to function properly,
But greed remains young for ever.'

" ' "The party reached the lake early in the morning.
The monkey chief said to the king, 'Your Majesty,
whoever enters the lake, when the sun has half risen,
gets the present, but everyone must go in simultaneously.
However, you can enter the lake at another place that
I will show you.'

" ' "So the king went off with the monkey chief and
everyone else went into the lake and was eaten up by
the Rakshasa.

" ' "When the others did not reappear, the king said
to the monkey, 'Oh, Monkey Chief! Why have my people
taken so long to come out?'

" ' "Then the monkey chief climbed up a tree and
addressed the king, 'Wicked King! Your court and the
members of your household have been eaten up by the

Rakshasa, who lives in this lake. You killed my family
and I have had my revenge on you. They say that it
is no sin to return evil for evil. Well, you annihilated
my race and I have destroyed yours. I saved you because
you were once my master.'

" ' "When the king heard this, he was throughly shaken
and returned on foot to his kingdom.

" ' "When the king had gone, the Rakshasa emerged
from the lake and said delightedly to the monkey chief,
'Well done, Monkey Chief! You have destroyed your
enemy, made friends with me and also acquired a
diamond necklace. By drinking water through a lotus
stem, you achieved everything you desired.'

— "And so," continued Suvaranasiddhi, "that's why I
said:

'A man who, overcome with greed,
    Does not think about the consequences,
    Will be put to scorn like King Chandra.'

— "And now, my friend, let me go home."

— "How can you go away and leave me like this!" said
Chakradhara. "They say:

'He who deserts his friends in distress,
    Shall surely go to hell.' "

— "That's true," said Suvaranasiddhi, "but only in a
case where you can be helpful. In your case, no human
being can do anything and I have no power to free
you. In fact; the more I see your face in pain from
that wheel, the more my heart tells me to get away
from here, as quickly as I can, in case same fate befalls
me. So, let me go home. You will have to stay here
and pay for your greed and for not listening to my
good advice."

— "You're right," said Chakradhara. "Go home."

And so, Suvaranasiddhi took his leave and left
Chakradhara to his fate.

THE END OF THE FIFTH TANTRA
AND OF THE PANCHATANTRA

GLOSSARY

A

Agnimukha: Fiery mouth.

Amaravati: A town in India.

Amarshakti: Eternal power.

Amavasya: When the moon is not at all visible.

Anagatavidhata: One who ponders over the solution of a problem before it arrives.

Anantashakti: Infinite power.

Anujeevi: Living on another's life.

Arimaradana: Destroyer of enemy.

Arjuna: Hero of the Hindu epic, *Mahabharata*. One of the five Pandava brothers. A great archer.

Ashadhbhuti: One born in the month of Ashadh, corresponding to June-July.

Ashrama: Hindu hermitage.

Avanti: A town in ancient India. Modern Ujjain.

B

Bahushakti: Great power.

Banyan: Indian fig tree.

Bath things: Towel, oil, perfume, etc.

Bhagawan: A polite expression used to address a scholar or a holy person.

Bhairavananda: Taking delight in Bhairava (Lord Shiva). Ananda is the suffix, used by persons who have renounced the world.

Bharatamuni: Renowned sage of ancient India who was the first to compile and write the musical systems of Indian music.

Bhasuraka: Terrible.

Brahma: Lord of Creation. According to Hindu philosophy, God is formless and has three aspects: Creation, Sustenance and Destruction. *Brahma* is the

Lord of Creation. *Vishnu* is the Lord of Sustenance. *Shiva* is the Lord of Destruction.

Brahmin: One of the four castes of the Hindus. In India, after the coming of Aryans, the society has been divided into four castes for the sake of efficiency and smooth running, so that the families took to the same profession. Thus the experience of a particular trade was handed down from father to son and so on. The following are the four castes in India. *Brahmins:* Their duty was to study and impart spiritual and educational instructions to the members of the society. They were supported by voluntary donations or by the kings. *Kshatriyas:* This is the warrior class. Their duty was to look after the defence of the country and also maintain law and order. *Vaishyas:* They are the tradets' class. Their duty was to see that the daily necessities of life were freely available at a reasonable rate. *Shudras:* This class used to work on the fields to produce food and also to serve the above three classes.

Nowadays the caste system is slowly disintegrating and there is no restriction to pick up the work of the other caste.

Brahmini: Wife of a Brahmin.

Brihaspati: Hindu name for planet Jupiter. Also according to Hindu mythology, name of a renowned sage who was the spiritual guide to the gods.

Brihatsphinga: Large buttocks.

C

Ceremony of the sacred thread: See Sacred thread ceremony.

Chakradhara: Holder of a wheel.

Chanakya: A great philosopher, economist, politician and diplomat of ancient India. Author of *Arthashastra*, a book on state politics.

Chandarava: Terrifying voice.

Chandra: Moon.

Chandrama: Moon.

Chandravati: Moon-like beauty.

Chaturadanta: Four tusks.

Chaturaka: Clever.

Chiranjeevi: Long life.

Chitragreeva: Spotted neck.

Chitranga: Spotted body.

Cobra: A poisonous hooded species of snake in India, called Naga which is worshipped in India only on Nagapanchami day and milk is offered to it.

Cowrie: Sea-shell. Used as currency in ancient India.

D

Dadhiputcha: Tail as white as curd.

Damanaka: Derived from Damana, which means to control, conquer or subdue.

Dantila: Strong teeth.

Deeptaksha: Shining eyes.

Devashakti: Power of gods.

Devata: Deity.

Dev Sharma: Name of a Brahmin.

Dhanadeva: God of wealth. In Hindu mythology, he is called Kuber.

Dharmabuddhi: Pious-minded.

Dhusaraka: Grey colour

Drona: The great Guru of the Pandavas and the Kauravas, referred to in the *Mahabharata*. Teacher of the martial techniques.

Durga: Goddess Durga. Also called Parvati, the wife of Lord Shiva.

E

Ekabuddhi: One talent.

G

Gandharva rites: Hindu love marriage, without religious rites.

Ganga: The river Ganges.

Gangadatta: Gift of the river Ganges.

Garuda: In Hindu mythology, he is referred to as Lord of the birds whom Lord Vishnu, the Sustainer of the world, uses to ride on.

Gem from the hood of a cobra: According to mythological belief, gems are also found in the hood of the cobra.

Gomaya: Cow-dung.

Gorambha: Bullock.

Guda: Crude sugar or jaggery.

Gujarat: An Indian State.

Gunja fruits: Red fruits resembling embers of fire.

Guptadhana: Buried wealth; stingy.

Guru: Hindu spiritual teacher.

H

Haridatta: Gift of Lord Vishnu, the Sustainer of the world.

Hiranyaka: Gold-like.

I

Indra: Lord of the heaven.

J

Jain Muni: A monk belonging to the Jain religion in India, founded by Lord Jinendra.

Jain religion: One of the religions practised in India, based on Ahimsa or non-violence.

Jalapada: Web-footed.

Jambu: Fruit of the Java Plum tree.

Jamnadatta: Gift of the river Yamuna or Jamuna.

Jinendra: Also known as Jina. Founder of Jain religion in India.

Jveernadhana: Completely using up wealth.

K

Kamadeva: God of Love. Also called Madan.

Kamandaki: Name of an ancient Nitishastra.

Kamatura: Passionate.

Kambugriva: Pot-necked.

Kanyakubja: Modern city of Kannauj in India.

Kapinjala: A species of game bird in India.

Karalakesara: Fierce mane.

Karalamukha: Ferocious mouth.

Karataka: Crow.

Khadira: Catechu tree. Used for producing fire in holy ceremonies. Extremely hard. Burns for a long time.

Kharanakhara: Sharp claws.

King of the three worlds: Heaven, Earth and the lower region of the world.

Kinshuka: Name of a red flower.

Kirata: A tribe in India that lives by hunting.

Krathanaka: Torn or cut.

Kravyamukha: Face like raw flesh.

Krikalika: Long throat.

Krurakarma: Doer of evil deeds.

Kruraksha: Cruel eyes.

Kuber: Treasurer of gods in Hindu mythology.

Kukudruma: Decorated tree.

Kulapati: Chancellor of an ancient Hindu educational institute.

Kusha grass: Holy grass used in religious rituals.

L

Laghupatanaka: Low flying.

Lakshmi: Goddess of wealth and beauty. Wife of Lord Vishnu, the Sustainer of the world.

Lambakarana: Long ears.

Lion's roar: A proclamation of an emphatic declaration that the speaker is absolutely right.

Lord Shiva: The Destroyer of the world.

Lord Vishnu: The Sustainer of the world.

M

Madotkata: Haughty.

Magha: Month of February.

Magic Wicks: In India, it is a common practice for holy men to pray over cotton threads or wicks and give them to their devotees who constantly carry them for good luck and protection from ill luck.

Mahachaturaka: Exceedingly clever.

Maharishi: A great seer, knower of truth.

Mahatma: A great soul.

Mahavira: Exceedingly brave. The name of the last of the 24 Tirthankaras (prophets or seers) of the Jains.

Mahilaropyam: As beautiful as a woman.

Mandaka: Baked dish made from flour, sugar and cocoanut.

Mandavisarpini: Slow-moving.

Mandavishya: Slow poison.

Manibhadra: Jewel of jewels.

Mantharaka: Slow-moving.

Mantra: Sacred words, whose constant repetition helps a person to concentrate on God. Also, words of enchantment used to overpower other people, animals, etc.

Manu: The author of the great law book, *Manusmiriti.*

Matha: Ashrama; Hindu hermitage.

Mathura: An ancient city in North India on the bank of the river Yamuna. Centre of pilgrimage for the Hindus. Associated with Lord Krishna who was born as an incarnation of Lord Vishnu, the Sustainer of the world.

Megha: Cloud.

Meghanad: Thunder.

Meghavarana: Colour like a cloud; dark.

Mendi. Henna. In India, on auspicious days, girls and women paint their palms and soles with this dye in beautiful designs.

Mitra Sharma: Name of a Brahmin.

Mountain Varuna: See Varuna.

Muni: A holy man of Jain religion.

N

Nala: A celebrated king of the Nishadas, hunters in India.

Nanda: Name of a great king in ancient India. Also name of the father of Lord Krishna.

Nandaka: Giver of pleasure.

Naraka: Hell.

Nitishastras: Ancient Indian moral scriptures about the proper conduct in life.

O

Om Namaha Shivaya: Om is symbol of. God; Namaha Shivaya means, bowing before Lord Shiva.

Ox without horns: Ridiculous or stupid.

P

Padmanidhi: A treasure.

Palasha tree: Kind of fig tree in India.

Palipura: A town in ancient India.

Pandavas: Five brothers mentioned in the great Hindu epic, *Mahabharata.*

Papabuddhi: Evil-minded.

Patliputra: A town in ancient India. Modern Patna.

Pingalaka: Reddish brown.

Prajeevi: Living on one's own efforts.

Prakarakarna: Straight ears.

Pralaya: End of the world.

Pratyutpannamati: One who ponders over the solution of a problem, when it actually arises.

Priyadarshana: Sweet face.

R

Raga and Ragini: A particular combination of the musical notes to give a particular melody. All Ragas have to be sung at particular fixed hours of the day. Some Ragas are based on seasons while others denote different moods of a human being.

Rakshasa: Demon.

Raktaksha: Red eyes.

Raktamukha: Red mouth.

Rama: Hero of the Hindu epic, *Ramayana.*

Ravana: The demon king of Lanka who was killed by Lord Rama, the incarnation of Lord Vishnu, the Sustainer of the world.

Ravi: Sun.

Rishi: A sage, knower of truth.

River Saraswati: A river in India named after Goddess Saraswati.

River Sipra: See Sipra.

Rshyamukam: Name of a mountain, near Pampa lake in south India.

Rukmapur: A town in India.

Rupee: Indian currency.

S

Sacred thread ceremony: A boy from only Brahmin or Kshatriya caste is privileged to undergo this religious ceremony before he is accepted by the Guru to his ashrama for studies. His head is shaved clean — only a tuft is left — and he is given a sacred thread for wearing on his body.

Sadhu: Hindu hermit, also used for persons who are too good and too religious.

Sagaradatta: Gift of the sea.

Sahasrabuddhi: A thousand talents.

Sanjeevi: Restored to life.

Sanjivaka: Medicine that revives one from death.

Sankata: Calamity.

Sankranti: A very auspicious day for the Hindus. On this day, the sun enters Capricorn, the house of the Saturn. Prayers are offered to Sun-god and sesame seeds distributed to express goodwill.

Sanyasi: A Hindu monk, who renounces everything for self-realisation.

Saraswati: Goddess of learning, music and beauty. Wife of Lord Brahma, the Creator of the world.

Satyavachana: Truthful utterance.

Shakini: Witch attendant of Goddess Durga.

Shalihotra: A great writer of veterinary science.

Shami: A species of tree in India. Considered to be holy by the Hindus.

Shandili: A sub-caste of Brahmins.

Shankukarana: Ears like wedges.

Shastras: Ancient scriptures on religion, science, arts, etc.

Shastri: Well-versed in Shastras.

Shatabuddhi: A hundred talents.

Sheeghraga: Fast-moving.

Shinvshapa: A species of tree in India.

Shiva: See Lord Shiva.

Shloka: Verse.

Shuddhapata: Clean white clothes.

Shukra: Short form of Shukracharya. *See below.*

Shukracharya: A great sage in ancient India. Preceptor of the demons.

Sindhu: The river Indus.

Sindhuka: Name of a tree.

Sipra: A river flowing through Ujjain in India.

Sister: A polite expression used to denote one's own wife as the listener's sister.

Smashana: A place where the bodies are burnt after death, according to the Hindu religion.

Soma Sharma: Name of a Brahmin.

Somilaka: Placid.

Sthirajeevi: Steady life.

Suchimukha: Needle-like face.

Sumati: Good sense.

Sutrika: A sweet noodles-like preparation, made out of sugar and butter (Ghee).

Suvaranasiddhi: Gift of gold.

Swabhavakripana: Miserly nature.

T

Tamal: Name of a tree in India, with a very dark bark.

Tamrachuda: Red hair.

Tantra: Systems of study.

Tapasvi: A person who undergoes severe penance to attain self-realisation.

Tata: Sire.

Teekshadaunstra: Sharp teeth.

Tittibha: Birds called Seven Sisters.

Trial by fire: A trial conducted in ancient India to find out if a person was guilty or not. He was made to walk barefooted on the burning coals. If his feet got scorched, he was considered guilty, otherwise not guilty.

U

Uddhata: Rude.

Ugrshakti: Savage power.

Ujjeevi: Coming life.

Ujjwalaka: Bright white clothes.

Upabhuktadhana: A man who enjoys his wealth.

Upper garment: It is a custom amongst the Jains, who are great followers of non-violence, to cover their face with upper garment to prevent possible killing of any bacteria, etc., in the air, while inhaling.

V

Vajradaunstra: Adamant teeth.

Vakranasa: Crooked nose.

Varakeerti: Famous.

Vararuchi: Name of a famous grammarian. One of the nine gems (wise men) at the court of King Vikramaditya, a renowned king in ancient India, who was known for his justice.

Vardhamana: Growth or increase.

Vardhamanaka: A kind of a pot or pot-bellied.

Vardhamanapura: A growing town.

Varuna: Name of Vedic god of water. Neptune. Also the name of a mountain.

Vatika: A kind of cake with holes in it, made out of rice and pulses.

Vayu: Lord of the wind.

Vedas: Ancient Hindu holy scriptures.

Veena: An Indian stringed instrument. Lute.

Veenarava: Sound of Veena.

Veenavaunsha: Bamboo flute.

Vihara: Monastery.

Vikata: Ugly or difficult.

Vinayavati: Modest.

Vishnu: See Lord Vishnu.

Vishnu Sharma: Name of a Brahmin.

Y

Yadava: Warrior clan of the *Mahabharata* epic.

Yadbhavishya: Trusting to luck.

Yadnyavalkya: Name of a great sage and philosopher in ancient India.

Yama: God of death.

Yamuna (Jamuna): A river in north India, which starts from the Himalayas and flows through Delhi and joins the Ganges in Allahabad.

Yogi: An ascetic or saint who has achieved self-realisation, or union with the Universal Soul.

Yudhisthira: Steady in war.